The Artist
as
Ecologist

Contemporary
Art and the
Environment

The Artist as Ecologist

Contemporary Art and the Environment

Filipa Ramos

LUND
HUMPHRIES

First published in 2025 by Lund Humphries

Lund Humphries
Second Home Spitalfields
68-80 Hanbury Street
London E1 5JL
UK

www.lundhumphries.com
info@lundhumphries.com

The Artist as Ecologist:
Contemporary Art and the Environment
© Filipa Ramos, 2025
All rights reserved

ISBN   978-1-84822-523-7
eBook (ePub)   978-1-84822-525-1
eBook (PDF)   978-1-84822-526-8

A Cataloguing-in-Publication record for this
book is available from the British Library

Copy edited by Michela Parkin
Designed by Wolfe Hall
Set in Mediaan by Dávid Molnár
and WH Aldine Mono by Wolfe Hall
Printed by Tallinna Raamatutrükikoda, Estonia

Lund Humphries' EU GPSR Authorised Representative
is LOGOS EUROPE, 9 rue Nicolas Poussin, 17000,
LA ROCHELLE, France
contact@logoseurope.eu

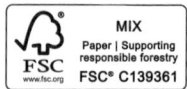

7   Foreword by Marcus Verhagen

9   *Introduction*
      One and Many Ecologies

20   *Chapter 1*
      Claiming

41   *Chapter 2*
      Returning

62   *Chapter 3*
      Performing

81   *Chapter 4*
      Reverberating

102   *Chapter 5*
      Exhibiting

124   *Conclusion*
      Art for the Present-Future

132   Notes

139   Further Reading

140   Index

143   Image Credits

144   Acknowledgements

NEW DIRECTIONS IN CONTEMPORARY ART

Series Editor: Marcus Verhagen, Senior Lecturer,
Sotheby's Institute of Art, London

A series of newly commissioned, engaging, critical
texts identifying key topics and trends in contemporary
art practice and discussing their impact on the
wider art world and beyond. The art world is changing
rapidly as artists avail themselves of new technologies,
travel ever more widely, reach out to new audiences
and tackle urgent issues, from climate change to mass
migration. The purpose of the series is to discuss
these and other changes, in texts that are accessible,
stimulating and polemical.

INTERNATIONAL SERIES ADVISORY BOARD

Foreword

Visit the website of Feral Atlas, a network of artists, anthropologists and scientists who trace the unintended ('feral') environmental consequences of human action, and you can see *Albatross* (2017), a film made by Chris Jordan on Midway Atoll in the Pacific. In it he shows clusters of brightly coloured objects, each sitting in a nest of feathers. These, it turns out, are albatross remains, the birds' flesh having decomposed to reveal the little scraps of plastic that they ingested as chicks and that eventually killed them.[1]

As we learn more about the climate crisis, pollution and biodiversity loss, through the news media but also occasionally through the work of artists like those in Feral Atlas, it is difficult not to despair.

The outlook today is even bleaker than it was when Jordan made his film. Disinformation campaigns, lobbying by the fossil fuel industry and other polluting businesses, the election of climate change deniers to positions of power, backsliding by politicians who once embraced green causes, poorly funded environmental projects: these and other developments have sapped faith in our collective ability to address ecological collapse. As Filipa Ramos says in the conclusion to this book, 'it is hard ... to continue longing for change when change itself has become synonymous with decay and not regeneration'.

And yet she consistently writes about artworks that militate against fatalism in their ingenuity, generosity and wit. In these pages we learn about seal rescue and spiders' webs, about experimental forms of pastoralism and the sounds of riverine life. We gain insights into the efforts of Indigenous peoples in Australia and Sweden to defend their lands and traditions. We are introduced to ancient forms of knowledge about – and saner ways of cohabiting with – plant and animal life. Most of the practices analysed here break with the overwhelmingly urban outlook and habits of the art world. Some are practical, others visionary, but all are potent sources of inspiration in the struggle against the devastation of the planet. Practices such as those discussed by Filipa have never been as relevant as they are today.

Marcus Verhagen

One and Many Ecologies

Art might have been born out of the sense that to be alive is to be in relation to oneself, to others and to the world: that to exist is to be part of a complex system in which each organism potentially affects all others. In this sense, artists have been ecologists since the beginning of time, using art to affirm their belonging to something larger than themselves and to share with others this connection to the land and the Earth. When studying prehistoric art, writer Lucy Lippard noticed how art, nature and society were intrinsically connected to one another, observing that, already at the dawn of history, art revealed how 'everything seemed to be connected to everything else'.[1] Some of the first artistic expressions ever made, palaeolithic paintings, reveal how humans represented themselves amidst the creatures that surrounded them, a togetherness that emerges from the motifs, supports and techniques they employed. All bodies were connected, their images and materiality assembled in a single surface. If the cave was the house that hosted these figurations for millennia, it later became the museum of a time in which people knew they were part of the land.

Contrastingly, the Anthropocene might also have been predicted by prehistoric art. Through the depiction of hunting scenes, individuals revealed their fascination for and desire to control and dominate other species. These images allowed the first humans to picture a different existence, in which they were separated from all other life forms. Thus, hunting and making art were also rituals of transformation, signalling the end of a planetary togetherness across humankind and other life forms that was just beginning and whose demise is today clearer than ever. Gradually, such control and killing of nature became the norm. This tension between the sense of being entangled with the natural world and the enactment of forms of dominance over other species reinforced human identity and its sense of supremacy. It is therefore clear that art participated in the project of consolidation of human exceptionalism, providing visions and supporting feelings that accentuated the divide between culture and nature and paved the way for extractivist and exploitative regimes. In this sense, art (in particular Western art) should acknowledge its contribution to the gradual constitution of the modern individual and its alienation from the natural world, visions that led to the current state of planetary crisis. But while this divide was becoming the norm, some continued making art as a way to think, feel and act differently. Their practices reflected a world whose ecological integrity was starting to be threatened, while renewing, through their gestures and forms, the awareness that to be human is to be part of nature.

This does not imply that art triggered the birth of environmental consciousness, the sense that nature (a concept so easy to address and so difficult to define), debilitated by human-led action, ought to be respected and cared for. Environmental consciousness emerged in connection with the reconceptualisation of ecology.

ECOLOGIES

Throughout the book, the term 'ecology' is related to artistic practices that are varied in genre and kind, naming those who embrace diverse forms of care for the planet as ecologists. It is important to acknowledge its different meanings, according to the traditions that have employed it. In the late 19th century, the German zoologist Ernst Haeckel (1834–1919) proposed ecology as a relational matter, arguing that 'by "ecology" we understand the comprehensive science of the relationships of the organism to its surrounding environment' (fig.1).[2] Despite the importance of Haeckel's definition, it did not take into

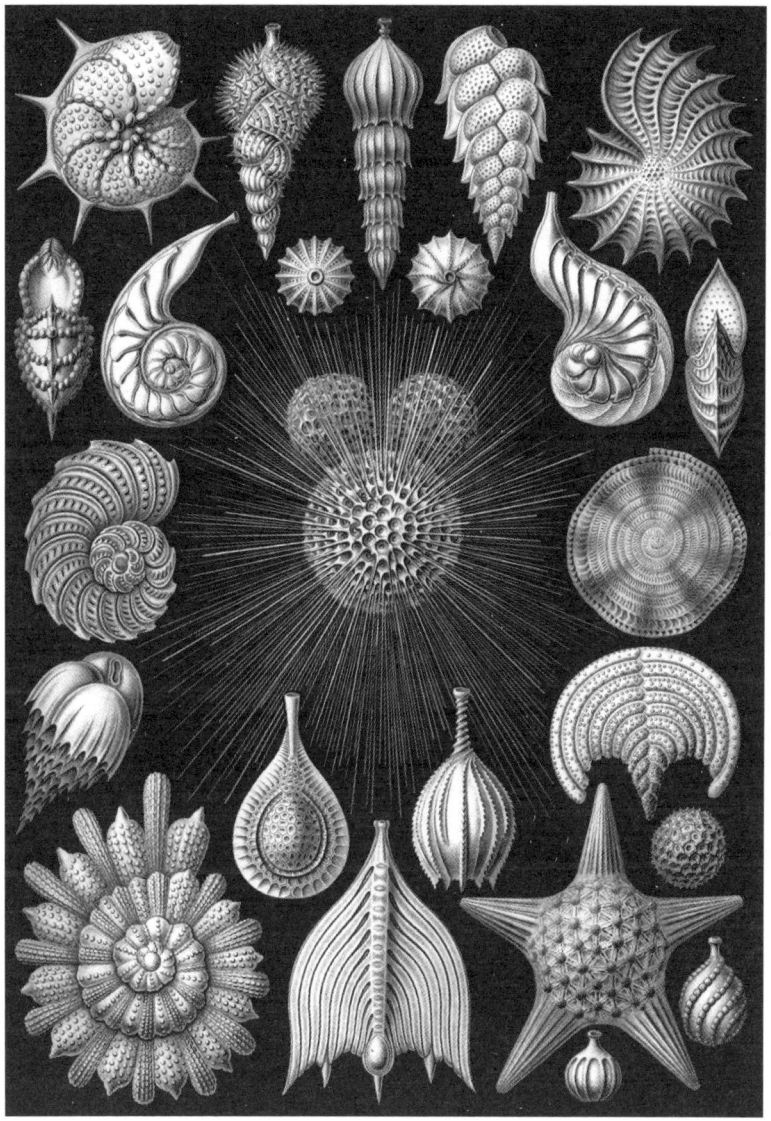

Fig.1 Ernst Haeckel, *Kunstformen der Natur*, 1904, plate 2: *Thalamphora*

account the anthropogenic context in which most organisms exist, ignoring how those relationships were affected, broken and conditioned by humans' interference with the world. It therefore may sound like a contradiction to focus on such action within a context that looks at artistic practices that attempt to heal the human-nature separation. It is likewise necessary to consider how this dogmatic chasm between humans and the natural world, enforced throughout the period of consolidation of modernity, affected organisms and environments, an awareness that also shaped renewed definitions and uses of ecology as a science and a practice. Indeed, this awareness – that the interaction between individuals, populations and spaces is in constant change, that it has been systematically conditioned by human action and that species and ecosystems do not only progress but are also exposed to decimation and extinction – placed contemporary notions of ecology in a terrain of concern, often connecting it to problem-solving missions. At a time of growing preoccupation with a world that is disappearing, which is connected to a sense of living in a permanent state of crisis, ecology became a matter of concern and care. The term was transformed and taken out of an academic and specialist context to give way to a movement of resistance and regeneration. Becoming a mode to mourn the dead, stay with the dispossessed and care for the resisting ones (human and nonhuman[3]), ecology started encompassing social and natural history and a series of non-disciplinary movements of imagination, love and concern for nature.

Affirming the importance of contemporary art in supporting the regeneration of a world that has been damaged and imagining alternatives to endless greed and consumption, this book introduces and discusses some of these artistic gestures of transformation. It sheds light on practices that attempt to repair and transform the mindsets that enabled the destruction of the planet. It avoids conceiving art as a toolbox or a set of solutions, which often only serve to maintain inherited ideologies concerning modes of occupation, production and consumption.

Instead, it stays with the complexity and opacity of art, celebrating its oblique methodologies and meandering expressions. It takes into account the forms in which the political, the poetic and the aesthetic are as entangled as those organisms that share an ecosystem.

ARTISTS AS ECOLOGISTS

The Artist as Ecologist is structured in five chapters that may be read independently but also unfold sequentially, following one another. Each chapter is named with a verb that encapsulates a possibility of transformation. Rather than reinforcing the feeling of despair, paralysis or nostalgia for a bygone world induced by the notion of climate crisis, all chapters debate positive struggles and action for and with the environment. *Claiming*, *Returning*, *Performing*, *Reverberating* and *Exhibiting* introduce art experiments of care for the planet that defy the representation and objectification of nature. They describe proposals which posit the transformation of our relationship with the natural world that still persists around and within ourselves. In doing so, these proposals also acknowledge that 'our' and 'we' are not homogeneous entities but complex denominations, in permanent change and reconfiguration, assuming diversity and recognising that trouble is common but shared unevenly.

While situated in the present, the artworks discussed here would not exist without the legacy of pioneering artists as ecologists, who advocated for a different way of living at a time in which these concerns were not as widespread as they are today. Fighting for a more equal society, these artists called for the abolition of gender and racial divides and for a smoother connection between people and nature, conceiving of social and environmental justice as implicated in one another. In fact, these artists understood, from early on, the impact of extraction, pollution and extinction and the necessity of deploying art to propose that other ways of living were not only desirable but possible too. Their strategies and approaches were varied, also transforming the making and presentation of art. Some highlighted and strengthened the ties between art, politics and the environment. Such was the case of Joseph Beuys (1921–86), whose environmental consciousness was often present in his performances, actions and sculptures. In 1980 Beuys cofounded the German Green Party (having previously expressed a trans-species view on politics, as when he declared that 'the German Student Party is the world's largest party, but most of its members are animals'[4]). A few years later, on the occasion of Documenta 7, the artist led the planting of 7000 oak trees in Kassel (*7000 Oaks*, 1982), proposing sculpture as a transform-ational, time-based art that exists in and for the world and beyond the limited duration of an exhibition. Many of the oaks Beuys planted can still be seen in the gardens and parks of the German city.

Other artists approached ecology from more technical standpoints. Such was the case of Nancy Holt (1938–2014), whose large-scale, outdoor *System Sculptures* were often placed in landfills and barren areas from which they activated air, water, fire and gas flows out of decomposing organic matter. Interested in astronomy and in ancient celestial references, Holt also aligned many of her pieces with sunrise and sunsets on the equinox and solstice, the North Star and the moon. Also occupying barren sites, often unoccupied roadside zones, Bonnie Ora Sherk (1945–2021) was interested in performative actions that reconsidered the species divide as well as the territories assigned to humans and animals. Her *Sitting Still* series, a set of performances she made during the 1970s, consisted in her sitting still, elegantly dressed, in unusual spaces such as garbage dumps, and transforming the perception of and consideration for a given environment with her simple presence.

If Holt and Ora Sherk stood out as women practitioners in a time still shaped by the attention given to white male artists, Ana Mendieta (1948–85) was instrumental in introducing ecofeminist stances in art. The artist's performative and film work, namely the *Silueta* series of performances for the camera that she made between the early 1970s and the early 1980s, documented her visceral interactions with land, sea and fire. Using film to explore the relationship between her own body and the landscape and to act as an agent of mediation between the elements, Mendieta also bridged the material and the spiritual world. As she mentioned in 1983, 'Now I believe in water, air, and earth. They are all deities. They also speak ... Those are the things that are powerful and important. I don't know why people have gotten away from these ideas.'[5]

Questioning individual identity and highlighting the interconnection of living and non-living matter, human-made objects and nature, Tatsuo Kawaguchi (b.1940) conceives his works as a permanent process of transformation, responding to time according to their own nature. Following the Chernobyl nuclear disaster of 1986, Kawaguchi started wrapping different materials, such as seeds, plants, soil and tools, in lead, which protects against radiation. In the 1960s Kawaguchi cofounded the collective Group 'I', whose members were nine Kobe-based artists interested in exploring the creative possibilities of impersonal collectivity, a transformative approach to the romantic conception of the artist as a single individual detached from the world, including nature.

GESTURES OF TRANSFORMATION

Following in the wake of these proactive, transformative traditions, the book is structured around five verbs that describe concrete artistic action. The first chapter, *Claiming*, deals with some of the most pressing debates of our current times, those concerning the shared rights of people and nature, and the equal treatment of different communities and their environments. This chapter looks at how contemporary art has provided an important terrain for the expression of those rights, functioning as a platform for encounter, support and outreach as well as a system where new languages and positions can be experimented with. *Claiming* is anchored around the activity of the Karrabing Film Collective, a group of inter-generational Aboriginal filmmakers from Australia's Northern

Territory who during the last decade have shown their work at major film and art institutions worldwide. The collective has been making films about how its members' lives are affected by governance, and which attempt to understand how to be socially and politically relevant for their communities through the collective practice of art. *Claiming* further discusses how artists address Indigenous and environmental justice through two other case-studies with a strong narrative weight. Through her weavings, in particular her monumental embroidery *Historjá*, Britta Marakatt-Labba narrates the environmental, political and mythological history of the Sámi peoples of the Northern Hemisphere. Her involvement in the early environmental struggles of her region and her depiction of the past and present of her land and people are debated here. The chapter also observes how the collective COUSIN has established an intergenerational network of American practitioners, supporting Indigenous artists working with moving images and sound while challenging aspects of exoticisation and self-representation that often traverse their own identities.

The following chapter, *Returning*, discusses the work of three artists who in recent years have embraced rural practices and engaged in farming and non-industrialised food production processes. Fernando García-Dory's initiative INLAND opens a reflection on the motivations and outcomes of artists who, like him, decided to embrace a life where agrarian and artistic methods are inseparable. Based in Spain and connected through an international network, INLAND is a community of farmers and craftspeople and a shepherds' school. *Returning* reflects on how García-Dory conceives activities such as beekeeping, cheese-making and organic farming as an integral part of his art. Considering two other initiatives that precede and have developed after INLAND, *Returning* also analyses how the work of other artists who have chosen to embrace a rural life is aesthetically meaningful and institutionally successful whilst also relying on important environmental acts. This is the case for Futurefarmers, a collective that activates systems of food trade and production in the United States

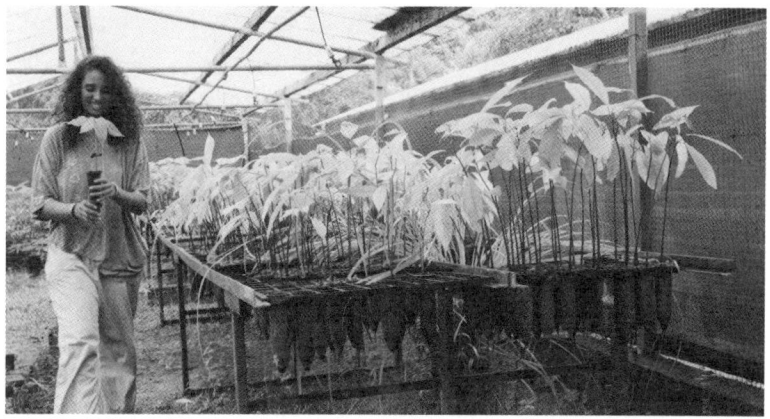

Fig.2   Artist Tabita Rezaire at the Amakaba cacao farm in the Amazonian forest of French Guiana, 2022

and Europe, and Amakaba, a women-led healing and cacao-production centre established by artist Tabita Rezaire in French Guiana's Amazonian rainforest (fig.2).

The two following chapters, *Performing* and *Reverberating*, comment on the renewed interest within the context of contemporary art for live, sonic and time-based media, namely performance, moving images and aural practices. *Performing* analyses how artists present live acts that combine performing bodies, new media and environmental concerns. The chapter focuses on Joan Jonas's project *Moving Off the Land* (2019), an audio-visual performance and installation in which the artist deals with the mythology and ecology of the oceans. Through this major work, Jonas expressed her ongoing interest in environmental matters that has appeared across her consistent depiction of and engagement with animals and landscapes and her collaboration with her companion dogs, thus providing an opportunity to reflect on how the growth of an ecological sensibility has concretely impacted upon the practice of such an important artist. *Performing* also looks at Rugilė Barzdžiukaitė, Vaiva Grainytė and Lina Lapelytė's *Sun & Sea (Marina)*, the opera that won the Golden Lion for the Lithuanian Pavilion at the 2019 Venice Biennale and that dwells on the contradictions of climate change in a compelling manner. Eduardo Navarro's F.O.C.A. project sees the artist behaving like a seal to help the recovery of baby orphan seals that reach the shores of Uruguay. While discussing the limits and possibilities of notions of becoming and transformation in art, the chapter concludes with this hopeful initiative that bridges ecological activism with performance.

Reverberating looks at how artists have used sound and music to capture and broadcast nature, discussing the ways in which they have chosen to explore non-visual realms to present the cries and echoes of a wildlife in peril. Central to the discussion is Tomás Saraceno's *Arachnophilia* community, a cross-disciplinary project that brings together artists, musicians, philosophers and scientists to study spiders and their webs. One of its public manifestations is a series of concerts and jamming sessions with spiders that attempt to explore matters of agency and create resonance across species. In dialogue with Saraceno's *Arachnophilia* are *Bestiari*, Carlos Casas's Catalan Pavilion for the 2024 Venice Biennale, and Jana Winderen's *The River* commission for London's Natural History Museum. Both Winderen and Casas spatialise field recordings of animals and environments and create complex sonic installations that transform space, occur in an extended duration and invite viewers-turned-listeners to engage with the natural world through sound and the unknown.

Pursuing an investigation of how artists relate to the format of the exhibition and understand their role within the institutional context of contemporary art, *Exhibiting*, the book's final chapter, analyses Pierre Huyghe's environmental installation *Untilled*, presented at Documenta 13 in Kassel in 2012, to anchor a debate that concerns strategies of display, exhibition and discourse in which nonhuman life, audiences and infrastructures constitute and influence one another in the creation of a novel ecosystem. *Untilled*'s fragility, permanent mutability and resistance to be documented challenge the format of the exhibition while inviting art contexts to accommodate complex living environments. The chapter further discusses the work of Feral Atlas, a collective of artists, anthropologists, architects and biologists initiated by anthropologist Anna Lowenhaupt Tsing and dedicated to documenting and interrogating the concept of ferality, which describes movements and transformations that, despite occurring on anthropogenic landscapes, escape human control. Feral Atlas has presented its research in several international shows, such as the 2018 Sharjah and 2019 Istanbul Biennials. Combining thoughtful displays that bring together scientific and artistic languages and contents, Feral Atlas invites institutions to rethink their roles, formats and narratives. Taking such considerations into the realm of the post-natural and bionic, the chapter also introduces Anicka Yi's *In Love with the World* (2021) at Tate Modern, an installation of flying, alien-like aerobes that pushes forward art's relationship with technological and environmental issues while enchanting visitors with figures that require little mediation strategies.

CROSSINGS

Beyond the linearity of these discussions, there are many threads that turn *The Artist as Ecologist* into a network of references and ideas that crosses the artworks and projects introduced. Various examples of grass-roots methodologies coexist with technological advances and activist struggles, while embodied approaches to ecological and sensorial attunement invite a new conceptualisation of institutional practices. In their difference and uniqueness, often acknowledging previous artists while moving forward the ecological engagement of art, they may embrace opacity, strangeness and the unknown. They challenge literal and figurative representations and suggest that the aesthetic, the poetic and the political are complementary realms. They all propose possible ways to break the spell that modernity has cast upon people, to reference writer Vanessa Machado de Oliveira – the naturalised belief that humans are separated from nature, contributing to the urgent revision of the single narrative of progress, which has inflicted so much damage upon the Earth.[6]

Chapter 1

Claiming

An iconic photograph (fig.3) immortalises the Alta River
protests, which took place in Norway between the end of the
1970s and the beginning of the 1980s. It is composed of two
strips of white landscape. The lower one features a grey river
calmly flowing below a snowy shore. Above it a soft, snowy
hill punctuated by skeletal vegetation extends itself until it
meets a milky sky. In between them, there's the human realm:
a group of civilians and Sámi people, identifiable by the bright
red and blue clothing they wear, are busy blocking an area
with rocks and a small, yellow bulldozer. Men holding film
cameras and microphones are amongst them. Taken in 1979,
this photo documents a moment in the decade-long mass
protest movement Folkeaksjonen [The People's Action], which
united Sámi and Norwegian activists against the Norwegian
government's project of building a dam in the Alta River,
in the north of the country. The movement gathered sympathy
and attention in Scandinavia and beyond, being supported
by local villagers, researchers from Norwegian universities,
and Indigenous and environmental groups.

Despite its failure to halt the construction of the hydro-
electric power plant, the Folkeaksjonen paved the way for
important political, environmental and artistic responses.[1]
Following the protests, the Sámi Rights Commission was
created in 1980. In parallel, the original dam project was revised
and downsized, preserving the village of Máze, which would
otherwise have been flooded. In 1978 a group of Sámi artists
founded the Mázejoavku [the Máze Group], a collective
dedicated to promoting Sámi art and culture whose workspace

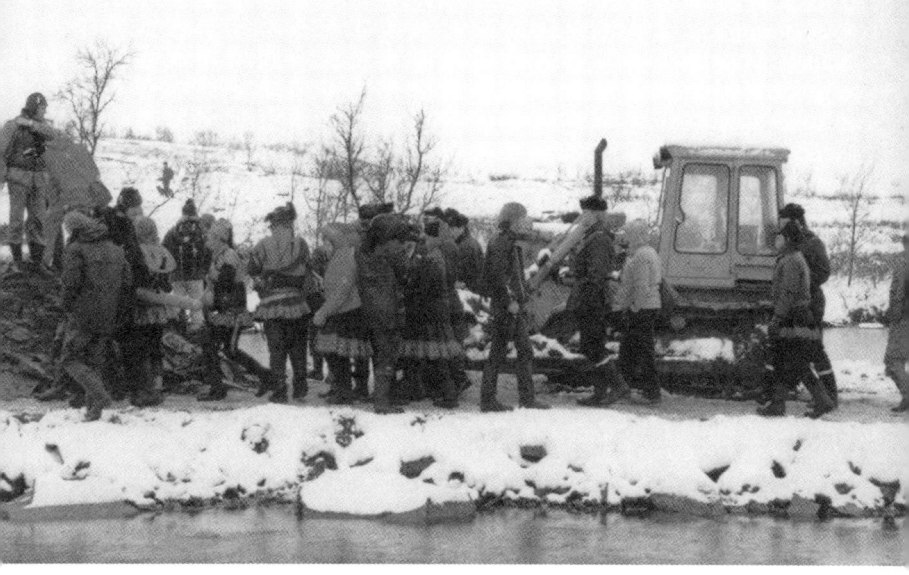

Fig.3   Blockade against the Alta hydroelectric project on traditional
Sámi territories, Stilla, Norway, 1979. National Archives of Norway, Oslo

hosted many of the protesters' gatherings. Britta Marakatt-
Labba, one of the artists discussed in this chapter, joined the
group in its early days. In her embroideries, humans, animals,
celestial beings and landscapes of the North are impossible to
disentangle. Her absorbing renderings of her people's struggles
continue, up to today, to support their rights and claims.

CLAIMING AMBIVALENCE

Titling this chapter, the verb *to claim* exposes the ambivalence
faced by many of those who turn this gesture into an artistic
expression. To claim is to demand recognition of a right
and to declare something as property. These two claiming
acts can conflict with one another: to express an entitlement
to something lost and to assert ownership over something
gained may be the cause and effect of a single event, as the
grief for the oppression of Indigenous culture and expropriation
of Indigenous land are connected by the ways in which these

were 'discovered' and reclaimed in the wake of settler-colonial agendas. As such, claiming acts in connection to Indigenous land ownership and occupation continue to shape some of the most pressing issues of our times. They are a fundamental, inaugural feature of the artist as ecologist, who fights for the rootedness of identity and who is aware of how social and land-rights activists fight side by side against the settler-colonial mentalities of the past and the future.

Intersecting social and environmental justice, *Claiming* observes how three Indigenous practices rely on the values that define their identity, and their ancestral and present-day connections to the land and its people, to respond to the world-wide distribution and perpetuation of inequality, exploitation and toxicity. Temporally, the chapter moves across a past that continues to haunt people's lives; it stays with practices of grief that help individuals and collectives to respond to present-time uncertainty with hope and imagination; and it envisages the possibility of a future where coexistence and repair are achievable. In tandem, it observes how Indigenous knowledge, aesthetics and experiences may be capable of mending a world that has been broken by selfish and careless actions while also challenging the sometimes-romantic views that indigeneity's duty is to launch wake-up calls to those who have stopped listening to science and nature, proposing that Indigenous methods are capable of prodigious healing.

INTERTWINING TIME, PLACE AND IDENTITY

The work of the artists and collectives considered here has had a significant importance in consolidating the presence of Indigenous claims in the institutional context of art during the past decade. The chapter is rooted in the activity of the Karrabing Film Collective, connected to the coastal areas of Australia's Northern Territory. It also incorporates the work of the North American Indigenous peoples' cinema collective COUSIN, constituted by artists Sky Hopinka, Adam Khalil,

Alexandra Lazarowich and Adam Piron. It concludes by looking at the work of Sámi artist Britta Marakatt-Labba, whose weavings incorporate the environmental, political and mythological history of the peoples of the Sápmi region in the north of Europe.

The activities of the Karrabing Film Collective, COUSIN and Marakatt-Labba are crucial to the debate about how contemporary art provides tools for social and environmental struggles, as well as how it functions as a space of encounter, debate and outreach and as a system where new languages and positions can activate transformation. The work of these three artists and collectives attests in unique ways to how art responds and reacts to how humans, nonhumans and the land have been dispossessed and exploited, by demonstrating the rights both of people and of nature. The plastic languages they adopt are original and poignant, be they the Karrabing Film Collective's highly-edited digital video from handheld cameras, which are then exhibited as video installations in museums and galleries; or Marakatt-Labba's traditional weaving techniques and precise details of people and landscapes, often presented as patches of a cultural identity that needs to be preserved; or COUSIN's short and feature-length films, which circulate in both cinemas and museums. Their common interest in cultural and environmental presentation is subsumed into their individual agendas, in which the Karrabing's depiction of a dystopic reality of Indigenous experience intersects with Marakatt-Labba's delicate fabulations of the concrete and cosmic North and COUSIN's questioning of the thresholds that divide life from cinema. In parallel, their stances and struggles elucidate different approaches towards the preservation of Indigenous life and reveal how fighting for the rights of a people comes with fighting for the rights of the land.

The Karrabing Film Collective is a group of inter-generational Aboriginal filmmakers from Australia's Northern Territory. They make films and installations that express how their lives are affected by colonial governance. Their work exemplifies how a collective practice of art may be socially and politically relevant for a community. Similarly, the collective COUSIN was founded with the mission to create an Indigenous film movement engaged in radical aesthetics and politics. Making work that merges but also defies genres and formats, bringing together artists from different generations and backgrounds and assembling traditions of literature, music and image-making, the members of COUSIN have proved how Indigenous claims walk hand in hand with the advancement and transformation of the languages of art and film.

Growing up in a family of Sámi reindeer herders in northernmost Sweden, Marakatt-Labba was an early member of the Máze Group, a collective dedicated to making Sámi cultural practices present within contemporary art. Primarily working with embroidery, Marakatt-Labba weaves miniature worlds where the environmental, geopolitical and mythological history and cosmology of her people are brought together. Her embroideries portray the life, rituals and struggles of the Sámi, who live across northern Norway, Sweden, Finland and Russia. The Northern landscape, which hosts the humans, animals and deities that traverse it, is a permanent presence in her work.

Together, these three practices intertwine questions of time, place and identity: they produce images that move and are in motion, which are conveyed by still and moving images. While the members of the Karrabing Film Collective and COUSIN make films, videos and installations, Marakatt-Labba's weavings tell the stories of her land and its inhabitants through detailed narrative sequences that participate in, but also complicate, the linear logic of time. If storytelling is a fundamental characteristic of all three cases observed, in their own way, they resist making art that illustrates their experiences and also defy the viewer's desire for participant observation, for direct immersion in their experiences. This is a fundamental aspect that brings together these three practices, aligning them with several others that are discussed across the whole book.

The Karrabing Film Collective is an Indigenous group formed by more than 30 members, most of them based in the ancestral coastal lands of Mabaluk and Bamayak, in the Northern Territories of Australia. In Emmiyengal, one of the traditional languages of the Karrabing members, 'karrabing' means the lowest point of the tide, when the ocean has receded, a moment that creates the occasion for collective gathering. Through its name, the collective (which will be named here as 'Karrabing', following the way its members refer to themselves) became a group defined by a temporal, contingent moment, a cyclical rhythm that regularly serves as an interface between land and sea, people and ocean, saltwater and freshwater. Its name expresses a connection to the land the group inhabits and the life forms which that land hosts and fosters. Its name is also a word that many of its audiences are not able to fully understand, as it is attached to an experience and place that to a large extent many people can only partially imagine. It is a name that carries several projections, expectations and imaginations, which the collective's films address, complicate but in the end do not clarify. This indiscernibility, this space between what is proposed and what may be felt, a space that exists beyond representation and within affective exchanges, may be one of the most remarkable features of Karrabing's work across art, activism and cinema.

The Karrabing Film Collective emerged in 2009, when its members realised that in order to receive funding to work on their territories, they would have to open them to resource extraction. This was not a novelty, but a matter that became particularly acute in that period, given the Australian Government's increase in control over Indigenous lives and lands, connected to a Northern Territory National Emergency Response Act approved by the Australian parliament to fight 'backward' Indigenous culture and to 'improve' and 'modernise' it through its stronger participation in the country's economy. This was to be achieved largely by participating in mining explorations and allowing their presence within their lands as one of the very few possible ways of accessing income.[2]

Facing this pressure and contradiction, Karrabing was formed with the hope that art would create a counterflow of analytic, material and ecological values. Karrabing has since brought life into art and art into life. Its films and installations emerge from experiences within the collective; they reflect their day-to-day lives, the stories they have grown up with and the narratives that inform their future perspectives. These are expressed through audiovisual experiments, videos shot on phones and handheld cameras that reveal the ancestral and present-day stories and imaginaries of its individual members and the collective as a whole.

DISRUPTING THE REAL WITH THE REAL

Karrabing's films and installations generally intersperse depictions of daily life with other-worldly events and fantastic characters. At first glance, these could be considered flash-backs to Karrabing's entanglement with the past and present, in which the colonial oppression of its predecessors still dictates – genetically, economically, geographically and affectively – the ways current lives are led. They could also be seen as moments of fictional disruption of the 'real', in which classic cinematic and fictional characters of fantasy and horror do what they do best, which is to reveal the porosity and the cracks in modernity's chasms between rationalism and animism, superstition and psychosis, science's histories and magic's mythologies.

In Karrabing's films and installations, mermaids lure young people (as in the collective's film *Mermaids, or Aiden in Wonderland*, 2018, fig.4), zombies attack children (*The Family*, 2021), resentful ancestors call for the punishment of the community (*Wutharr, Saltwater Dreams*, 2016), welfare representatives flirt with abusive laws (*When the Dogs Talked*, 2014), the ghosts of British explorers haunt the people they dispossessed and white people 'suck the life' of children (*Night Fishing with Ancestors*, 2023). On an initial reading,

THE ARTIST AS ECOLOGIST

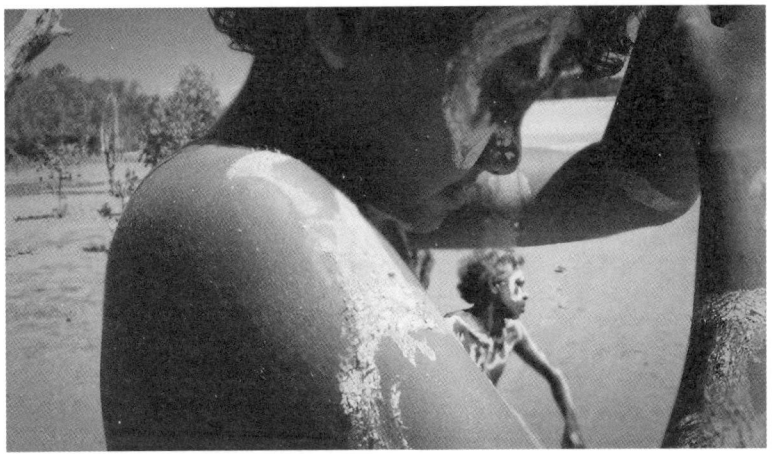

Fig.4 Karrabing Film Collective, *Mermaids, or Aiden in Wonderland* (still), 2018

these characters and situations could be seen as metaphors for the struggles, fears and systemic inequality Karrabing members are exposed to. Yet, what the films and installations show is that these hallucinatory moments and figures are intrinsic to Karrabing's existence. They are as constitutive of their relationship to their surroundings as those moments that seem to be untouched by what to a Western reading may be seen as psychedelic fantasy. Through this porosity between bare community life and the revengeful call of monstrous figures, the films and installations dialogue with the logic of the horror genre movie (relying on the activation of mechanisms that trigger anticipation and fear based on the viewers' knowledge that the worst will always happen) only to reveal how Karrabing's members' lives – even in the most mundane moments, day and night, within and outside the domestic environment (the house being such a classic site for suspense), in the past and present – are permanently exposed to toxic, violent and dangerous agents, both human and nonhuman.

The collective has also embraced other genres in its work, namely the format of the videoclip. This compelling tool for condensed, effective and mnemonic storytelling is integrated within Karrabing's narrative, further breaking it up while contributing to its fluidity. In the video installation *Forward with the Ancestors: Day in the Life* (commissioned for the 13th Gwangju Biennale in 2021), a hip-hop song with the refrain 'Forward to the bush, but where's he gonna go?' is repeated at key moments. It establishes a transcultural alliance across traditions of musical and creative response to dispossession and anger while empowering Karrabing communities with energy, words and sounds of resistance. Sometimes sound infiltrates and permeates viewers' bodies, almost like a spell. The short film *Wutharr, Saltwater Dreams* contains an even more effective earworm device, performed by a group of revengeful ancestors who call for punishment. 'Punish them! Punish them!', they cry repeatedly with thin, furious voices that take over the listeners' minds.

IMPROVISATIONAL REALISM

Karrabing member Elizabeth A. Povinelli, Franz Boas Professor of Anthropology and Gender Studies at Columbia University in New York, is the sole white person in the collective. She often functions as an intermediary between her Karrabing family and peers, the institutional system of art where Karrabing often presents its work and gathers funding from, and the academic apparatus in which she also moves. Her participation in Western academia and her theoretical work influence the fact that she is often the group's spokesperson, but the individual accounts of other Karrabing members in interviews and podcasts also abound.

Povinelli describes the group's way of self-representation as 'Improvisational Realism', a method that brings together the narratives that convey the life, viewpoints and imagery of its members and a system to rearrange and retell history.[3] In parallel to the inclusion of fantastic creatures, the depiction of how infrastructural, economic and political obstacles shape Karrabing's daily routines is sometimes intercut with archival radio and television footage that conveys, through the words and voices of others whose viewpoints are revealed within their own settings, the historic layers of colonial abuse and dispossession they are exposed to. These moments are as horrifying as any zombie, ghost, toxic agent or mermaid ever figured by Karrabing, both because they are more real and more haunting. They reveal a temporal extension in which the past keeps complicating the present and messing up the future. By assembling registers from different times and media, the collective shows how its present and future cannot be disentangled from its past.

DISTORTIONS AND DECONSTRUCTIONS

Taking into account the circulation of Karrabing's work, which has been widely exhibited internationally through retrospectives in major art galleries and at film festivals, it is worth investigating how much the average visitor may grasp of the full complexities that are conveyed by their films, including the experience of being haunted.[4] Acknowledging how anthropology has attempted to build an understanding of Indigenous life and thought while also being profoundly implicated in the edification of the colonial project – by providing theoretical, philosophical, political, fictional and pedagogical tools that made settler-extracto-colonialism imaginable, desirable and possible – Karrabing has been counteracting the discipline's early links to colonialism and turning it inside out. If it was possible to conceptualise dominance, it should also be possible to dismantle it, and to gradually build up a different understanding of relations. How? By distorting one of anthropology's fundamental tools, that of using moving images to capture how people live.

Karrabing artists make movies by themselves, of, with and about themselves. They make these films for themselves, as a pedagogical tool to transmit their memory and histories, and for others. But these films don't merely portray and document problems, relations and environments. They are confusing, disorienting and hallucinogenic. The stories they tell do not follow a linear narrative. They are situated and outlandish, layered and dense. They are permanently traversed by flows of people, affects and realms. Everything is in motion, yet nothing is really captured. But these films do things. As Elizabeth Povinelli has said, 'in acting, the collective goes beyond belief, they create a mechanism to maintain land relations ... we all knew these stories, but they were hanging from a thread, and the making and repurposing of these films thickens a no to a settler voice and finds different ways to activate and reinforce relations.'[5] Filmmaking becomes a form of empowering and consolidating a memory and of attesting Karrabing's own way of being in the world.

Another way in which Karrabing's films contribute to disassembling anthropology's engagement in white settler colonialism's propagation of inequality is by deconstructing the instrumentalisation of knowledge in order to exert control. Karrabing's films don't portray people and places: they are strange and confusing; the stories they tell are hard to follow and viewers can easily feel lost in time and in a landscape that is so layered that it is unreachable. What one senses is much more concrete than what one comprehends. While speaking about the sound of a pelican that can be heard in one of the films, Povinelli said, 'it doesn't really matter if the audience knows what the sound of a pelican is'.[6] She makes it clear that it is not that relevant if audiences understand Karrabing's films or not, for their role is not to render its members' experience accessible, or to make their life easily comprehensible for a global audience. Povinelli observes:

> the density of narrative flow and across a linguistically unexplained pattern of sound and visual semiotics may produce a limit-experience for viewers; a being left alone with their incompetence. Various affects may arise from this limit-experience, various thoughts may pass through viewers' minds: 'I couldn't understand what they were saying-doing'; 'I wish I could understand what they were saying-doing'; 'Why didn't they explain what they were saying-doing *for me*?'[7]

The relationship between the powerful, compelling modes of storytelling of Karrabing and their opacity guarantees the collective its independence, agency and transformative possibility. While Karrabing creates the conditions to welcome and incorporate viewers in exhibition settings – as when it includes used tyres for viewers to sit on in the installation of *Forward with the Ancestors: Day in the Life* (2020) – it seems to resist exposing what belongs to the community. Povinelli continues:

> the resource extraction against which Karrabing stands is not merely mining – fracking, mineral, water mining – but epistemological mining. Thus, within Karrabing films ... is a dynamic of the occluded, alluded and foreclosed said, seen, and heard ... The difference [is] between who is expected to give away everything they have in order to be given even the smallest grip within white settler colonialism and who must do more than sit back and wait to be enlightened.[8]

By enacting these processes of denial and making films and installations that are strange and unfathomable to many, especially Western audiences, Karrabing rehearses and experiments with forms of empowerment that, in an important twist, rely on its members' Indigenous identity to bypass the stigmas and oppressive regimes which that identity is exposed to.

COUSIN'S CALL

Questions surrounding matters of exposure, opacity and contextualisation also frame many of COUSIN's interests and concerns. As a collective that defies conventional formats of organisation and promotes the making of experimental films and artworks by Indigenous individuals, its members are constantly confronted with the definition and purpose of Indigenous cinema. Their work moves forward the investigation of what indigeneity means today, both for Indigenous and non-Indigenous people. COUSIN was founded in 2018 by four US-based artists and filmmakers descending from North American

Indigenous peoples: Sky Hopinka (Ho-Chunk Nation / Pechanga Band of Luiseño people), Adam Khalil (Ojibway), Alexandra Lazarowich (Cree) and Adam Piron (Cáuigù and Kanien'kehá:ka). They were all together during that year's Flaherty seminar, a week-long, annual programme of screenings and talks by and for experimental cinema artists, scholars and professionals, held in Colgate, Upstate New York. As they explain, 'the question of how to find other Indigenous filmmakers who are making work that is experimental and exciting was where we began'.[9]

Defying conventional formats that make a clear distinction between what an artistic collective, a production and distribution company and an advisory office are, COUSIN appears as a solidarity network created by and for Indigenous artists working with moving images. Its mission to 'build an Indigenous cinema movement' has been successful. Through annual support cycles, initiated in 2020 during the pandemic, it helped an important number of practitioners, Indigenous individuals and collectives, whose work has been widely circulated and received critical acclaim in relevant art galleries and film festivals. Alongside their origins, what these artists also have in common is their investment in making work whose language and imaginary are unique and radical, non-illustrative, provocative and savvy of the traditions of avant-garde and experimental art, which they contribute to advancing in meaningful, urgent ways by embedding their artworks in non-white aesthetics and perspectives.

Refusing to reinforce the tropes associated with the spectacle of native communities, which for too long had to auto-exoticise themselves and reinvent representation modes they previously saw being denied and erased, these artists use their work to investigate what it means to be seen without having to perform oneself. This makes it clear that what is relevant and not, visible and not, understandable and not, centred and not largely depends on the perspective and point of departure of the viewer. Thus, the extent to which an Indigenous film collective also takes its audiences into account becomes of great importance. Similarly to Karrabing's work, the films, installations and moving-image artworks that emerge from COUSIN do not contextualise, explain or dissect Indigenous history for non-Indigenous eyes. But they can also be more abstract than those of Karrabing, as when they immerse viewers into intense experiences and abstract sensorial realms that allow them to feel more than understand. This is the case with the disorienting views of colourful fruiting cactuses pulsating to the rhythm of an improvised percussion in the short film *Coyolxauhqui* by the Mexican Colectivo Los Ingrávidos and with the abstract composition *Voiceless Mass* by the Diné artist Raven Chacon, thanks to which he became, in 2022, the first Native American composer to win the Pulitzer Prize for music.

As Hopinka has said:

> What does it mean to have facts about something or a culture or a community? And as I try to not explain things, I'm hoping that through context or the things that are nearby, an audience will be able to understand how I feel about them, or place themselves in a certain empathetic space where they may not know what's going on, but they know how to feel about it.[10]

Hopinka makes films that explore his Ho-Chunk Nation and Pechanga Band of Luiseño ancestry and attest to how people, language, land and sound shape one another. Music plays a fundamental role in his films and installations, as it does in Chacon and the Colectivo Los Ingrávidos's work. So does language, be it in English, in which he writes his texts and visual poems; Chinuk Wawa, an idiom from the Pacific Northwest that he studied and taught; or Pechunga, which connects him to his family. In Hopinka's short film *Kicking the Clouds* (2021, fig.5), viewers are offered glimpses of the artist's family history and current life, introduced by his grandmother's voice learning Pechunga from her own mother and then guided through his mother's recollections of her early years. While the two women are never visible, their voices are accompanied by footage shot in Whatcom County, Washington State, where

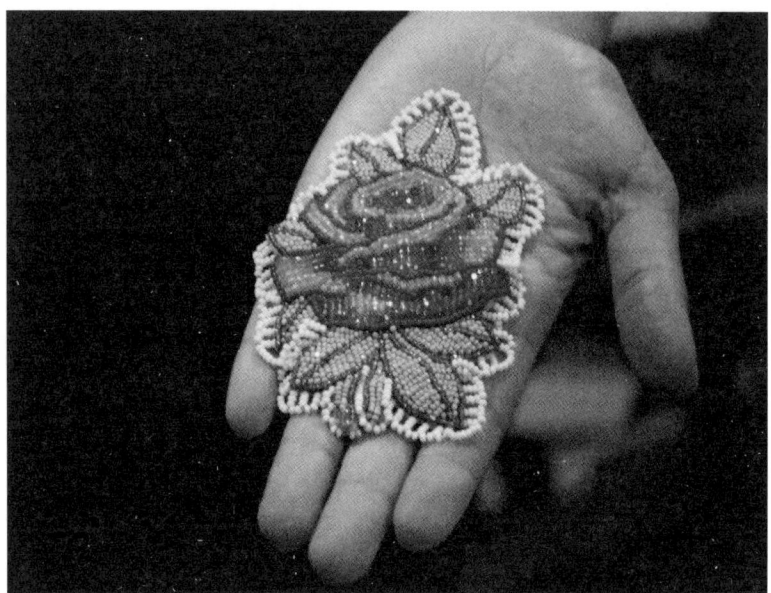

Fig.5   Still from Sky Hopinka's film *Kicking the Clouds*, 2021

the family still lives. In it, children and adults play on deserted beaches, hands manipulate delicate beaded objects, shots of forest and vegetation and endless, cloudy skies offer glimpses of a life that, even if being revealed, remains unfathomable.

CHALLENGING DOMINANT KNOWLEDGE

Other films made by founding members of COUSIN assume a more outlandish direction. This is the case with Adam Khalil and Bayley Sweitzer's feature film *Nosferasta: First Bite* (2021). Reframing the figure of the vampire within the context of the Western colonial project (a strategy aligned with Karrabing's engagement with classic horror film characters), Khalil and Sweitzer's *Nosferasta* follows the past and present lives of Oba, a Brooklyn-based artist and musician originally from Port of Spain, Trinidad, who also co-authors the film. Forcibly sent from West Africa to the Caribbean, where he is bitten by Christopher Columbus (who is featured as a vampire),

Oba is condemned to eternal loyalty to the colonial project, until an encounter with Rastafarianism breaks his spell. Aligned with Latinx professor Vanessa Machado de Oliveira's proposal that Western modernity cast a spell on people, 'keeping us in an immature state', and her call to hospice it (that is, to offer palliative care to a dying modernity), *Nosferasta* – and COUSIN's films in general – suggests that affects, rituals and non-Western epistemologies that challenge dominant forms of owning and retaining knowledge may effectively operate a process of individual and collective rewiring from the colonial narrative of progress.[11]

BRITTA MARAKATT-LABBA'S DOCUMENTING EMBROIDERY

Coming from a parallel history of colonial occupation, this time connected to the European context, Britta Marakatt-Labba was born in 1951 in the wake of the Second World War in Idivuoma, a part of Sápmi territory under Swedish jurisdiction.[12] The Municipality of Kiruna (Giron in Sámi), where Idivuoma is located, has been haunted by its own mineral richness. Its iron ore, the major mineral resource identified until recent years, has been systematically mined since the late 19th century. During World War II, Kiruna was a key geopolitical site, as several of its mines were in German hands while Swedish companies continued to sell even more iron to Germany to support the Nazi expansion. Today, it is known that the area around Kiruna hosts Europe's largest deposit of rare earth metals, essential to feed the surge in electric cars and wind turbines and support the European Union's efforts to be economically autonomous. The entire city of Kiruna, which was built at the end of the 19th century to serve the original iron-ore mine, is currently being relocated to a nearby area, as mining-related subsidence is putting at risk its buildings and infrastructure.[13]

Growing up in such a context and in a family of Sámi reindeer herders, in her early adulthood Marakatt-Labba moved to Gothenburg, in southern Sweden, to study textile art. Upon her return in the late 1970s, she joined two artists' collectives whose actions were fundamental to ensure the current recognition of Sámi's cultural expressions: the previously mentioned Mázejoavku and the Sámi Dáiddajoavku [Sámi Artists' Group]. During this time, Marakatt-Labba began using embroidery to make art. It did not take long for her cultural identity and political awareness to emerge in her work, as she employed this technique, conventionally associated with domestic crafts and female labour, to depict the struggles, practices and beliefs of her community and to celebrate the uniqueness of the Sápmi land and beings.

A MURDER OF CROWS

Through her embroidery, Marakatt-Labba has documented important historical events, such as the campaigns to prevent the construction of the hydro-electric power plant in the Alta River, which she depicted in *Garjját* [The Crows] (1981). Evolving like a graphic novel, the embroidery figures a murder of crows flying across boreal white skies. Gradually, the crows' wings are turned into black capes and their beaks into long noses. When they reach the ground, they have shapeshifted into Norwegian police agents, running to placate a group of protesters. Marakatt-Labba recalls that while she 'sat there demonstrating against this, all these policemen came over the mountain. Suddenly I remembered my mother's words about crows, that crows are like the authority, when they come to a place, they will take everything they will see ... For me these policemen were like crows because they came to Alta and took every single demonstrator and drove us to jail.'[14]

This scene of interspecies power and evil echoes another important feature of Marakatt-Labba's imagery: the representation of the religious and spiritual sphere of the Sámi. As curator Anders Kreuger notes in his analysis of the work, this 'metamorphosis-in-flight we just saw performed may also be a manifestation of ancient beliefs'.[15] Indeed, the becoming-policeman of the crows can also allude to the therianthropic

THE ARTIST AS ECOLOGIST

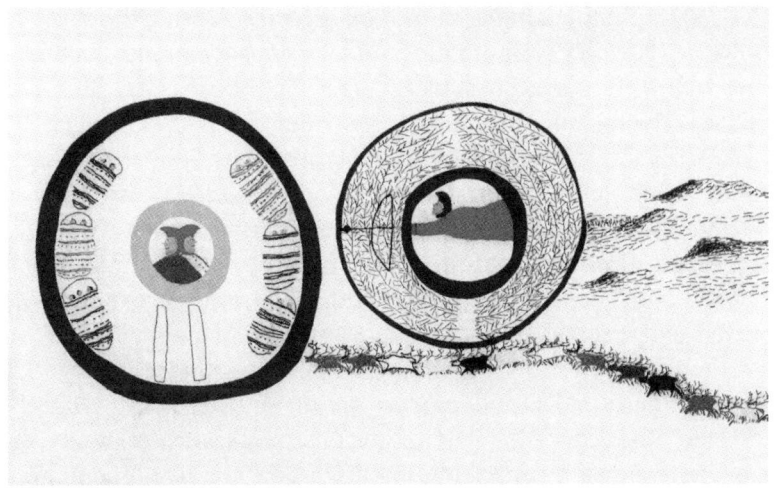

Fig.6   Fragment of Britta Marakatt-Labba's embroidery
Historjá [History], 2003–7

abilities of Sámi *noaidi* (shamans in Northern Sámi language).
Deemed pagan idolatry, shamanism and other Sámi religious
practices were made illegal and eradicated by Scandinavian
authorities from the 16th century onwards. Countering such
centuries-long denial of Sámi rights and the erasure of their
material and immaterial culture, Marakatt-Labba weaves
back their landscapes and cosmologies while revisiting and
imagining their environmental, geopolitical and mythological
histories. This is particularly visible in her major work so far,
Historjá [History] (2003–7, fig.6), a 79-foot-long embroidery
and collage that took four years to make and was commissioned
by the Arctic University in Tromsø, Norway.

Historjá portrays the life, rituals, struggles and daily life of
Sámi people and reveals how they are shared with local animals
and divinities (see fig.20). Resembling a long wall tapestry made
of cloth or an Asian paper scroll, *Historjá* functions like a long
march. Its characters and scenes unfold in a linear manner,
revealing themselves at the pace of the visitor walking alongside
it. Yet several events happen at once, and this simultaneity of
narratives is aligned with the uses that the Karrabing and some

COUSIN members make of motion pictures. Unlike them, however, *Historjá* is immobile, and viewers have to move along it to follow the scenes it depicts. Walking, they traverse and observe the forests, skies and water courses of Sápmi, as well as its urban dwellings and infrastructures. The final areas of fabric are left empty, without any embroidery. This emptiness becomes the winter snow of the boreal landscapes, but also the fragments of history and the connections between peoples that have been broken, obliterated, erased. This emptiness is spatial, meteorological and symbolic, but also political and concrete, for the Sámi are still struggling to reconstruct their identity between marginalisation, modernisation and self-exoticisation.

Here, the Sámi's ancient and fragmented tradition of storytelling as a historicising impulse and a creative mnemonic device meets an equally ancestral human propensity to conceive longitudinal supports – parietal friezes, paper scrolls, wall frescoes – as narrative systems. One of the most remarkable features of *Historjá* is that it demands that other spatial configurations be taken into account. If a single line dominates the composition, there are moments in which various actions happen across parallel axes, namely when blue, red and yellow knots and spheres holding goddesses and other-worldly beings appear and challenge the linear sequence of time. In an inch or two, the earthly context gives way to the celestial and then takes viewers into the underworld, as if it were not times but realms that were being traversed – a true shamanic journey that carries viewers with it, towards other forms of seeing and being.

Historjá was presented at Documenta 14 (2017), an event that contributed to Marakatt-Labba's long-due recognition, as well as that of the other seven Sámi artists – Máret Ánne Sara, Synnøve Persen, Keviselie [Hans Ragnar Mathisen], Mette Henriette, Iver Jåks, Niillas Somby and Joar Nango – who were part of the exhibition, which took place between Kassel and Athens. While celebrating this event, Katya García-Antón – at the time Director of Office for Contemporary Art Norway (OCA) and a driving force behind the Sámi presence in Documenta – reflected on how much still needed to be done:

THE ARTIST AS ECOLOGIST

What is essential is not how to react to Indigenous people, but how to engage with a history of colonialism in which Norway and the Nordic region have been entangled for centuries, and to comprehend that the image of Norway abroad as a beacon of social justice and as a political mediator does not correspond to the reality at home. The art world has an ethical imperative to decolonise.[16]

AN ETHICAL IMPERATIVE TO DECOLONISE

This imperative is shared by the members of the Karrabing Film Collective and COUSIN and the claims that their works assert. While generous and rich, offering moments of outstanding beauty that speak to a sensibility and understanding that exist beyond history, places and words, their works demand as much as they give to their audiences, and this is one of their most remarkable features. As daring as they are compelling, they contribute to a contemporary redefinition of what it means to claim one's identity and support one's kin and land: beyond illustration and explanation, refusing facile stereotypes, they linger in an opacity that is formal (blurred, scratched and overlayed images in the case of the Karrabing Film Collective and COUSIN, bearing large patches of white, empty fabric in Marakatt-Labba's works) and conceptual, as they refuse to let their art represent the role assigned to an identity. They also refuse to offer a monolithic view of the Indigenous experience.

Similarly, these artists reject appeals for self-exoticisation and stereotyped modes of representation, aware of how tradition may be a drive towards preservation but also a system of keeping relationships and societal structures in place, preventing political and social change, participation and emancipation. Enmeshing ancestral and contemporary references, languages, sounds and modes of representation – for instance, by combining Aboriginal claims with hip-hop music, as Karrabing do in the video *Forward with the Ancestors* – these artists refuse and defy stable, jargonised imageries and projections. The relationship they claim to their people and lands is not nostalgic but permanently actualised, as when Marakatt-Labba turns crows into present-day policemen and combines Sámi goddesses with activists in her embroidery *Historjá*. Forms of storytelling are updated and reinvented, as when COUSIN's Khalil and Sweitzer reframe settler-colonialism through a story of past and present-day vampires, blending reality and symbolism in their film *Nosferasta*.

Through the radicality and originality of forms, languages and methods used, these artists and collectives are fully integrated within the institutional system of art. While their works emerge from within specific contexts and are strongly connected to their makers' respective cultures and identities, they are widely exhibited. They are shown in individual and group exhibitions concerning both Indigenous and non-Indigenous matters in contemporary art museums, galleries and art fairs and in local and international film festivals. This porosity is a recent achievement, and one that should not be taken for granted, for if it has helped institutions to finally address their inclusivity quotas in exhibitions and collections, it should allow the access to institutional representation to continue to expand.

The concerns about the institutional integration of Indigenous and local practices are further debated in the following chapter, *Returning*, which will consider parallel, and often aligned, movements to and relationships with the land, specifically connected to non-urban, rural contexts. The chapter will discuss parallel struggles to challenge nostalgic conceptions of land use and occupation; to defy the idealisation, but also stigmatisation, of the rural context, its workers and inhabitants; and to question the logics of centre and periphery concerning art production and outreach. If in *Claiming*, matters of belonging, identity and sovereignty were mostly at stake, *Returning* will centre food production and distribution means, and how these are tackled by art practitioners.

Chapter 2

Returning

By being titled *Returning*, this chapter may suggest a sense of nostalgia, of coming back to something or someone, a movement that chronologically is more affiliated to the revisitation of the past than with the imagination of what is yet to come. By being used to address the ways in which artists and artistic collectives have adopted creative modalities for living and making art beyond urban settings, the verb may also imply that these individuals and groups, rather than moving forward and contributing to an advancement in the arts, opted to extract themselves from the system they once belonged to, turning their backs on the city to find refuge in a bucolic embrace of the countryside. *Returning* could therefore suggest that those engaging with rural practices have exchanged the progressive rat race of the metropolis for the harshness of rural settings and that they are now isolated, remote, but healthily detached from the alienating logic of urban cultural production.

Returning will indeed be used to describe the choices of artists who willingly challenged their practices and put them in dialogue with processes of food-making and communitarian life, activating dynamics of exchange between rural and urban environments – artists who decided that a more profound connection between the environment, our bodies and those of other species, and our systems of collective organisation for the production and distribution of food, could be achieved through the mindset and experimental methodologies of art. Yet, the verb *returning* is also used to question associations between the rural and the bucolic that perpetuate an imagined and idealised conception of the rural as a space of social segregation, romantic detachment and perfect ecological consistency. Considering how to return is also to give back and reciprocate, to transmit and deliver; the verb is employed to describe attempts to connect time and place, temporality and landscape, infrastructure and organisation. In Portugal, where I am from, to return, *revolver*, also means to plough, so I consider that the verb also has the potential to describe physical work with the land. If we consider that the Portuguese word for soil, *terra*, also means homeland and Earth, the notion of *revolver a terra*, turning up the earth, opens itself to wider possibilities that connect the ground, the place of origin and the planet.

In this *returning*, the concrete materiality of the soil being prepared for its cultivation, the turning of the heap, meets with the dreams of a revolution in how people inhabit the land, relate to the ground and engage with the planet: a revolution that revises the efficiency and productivity paradigms of contemporary food production, which have led to the profound damage inflicted on the environment by the agro-industry, namely through agro- and petrochemical dependency, intensive livestock-rearing and the associated habitat depletion for wild species. Within this context, artists become ecologists by embracing and experimenting with practices of care for the land that challenge the standards and stereotypes associated with the rural context and foster its relevance in terms of global cultural input. Art offers tools to merge social, land and environmental justice. It also contributes to challenging procedures and connects and reverberates culture and agriculture, care and creativity, labour and dissemination, combining questions and desires with concrete gestures of transformation that generate ways for the rural and the artistic to return and revolutionise one another.

RE-RETURNING

Albeit sharing the recognition of the connection between natural territories and resources and Indigenous and autochthonous people with the practices discussed in *Claiming*, here the attention turns towards modes of artistic revalorisation of rural cultures and non-invasive agricultural and food-production systems. Forms of artistic engagement with the land and within rural contexts are not a novelty of the current times of environmental concern. Beyond the well-known actors and artworks of Earth and Land Art – which emerged from the conceptual and performance art experiments, institutional critiques and environmental sensibilities of the mid-1960s – there has always been a strong relationship between art and the natural and rural contexts.[1] This relationship preceded and resisted the polarisation of the cultured agora and the 'agricultured' countryside. It also anticipated the changes brought about by the Industrial Revolution, following its journey towards urbanisation and globalisation.

In her book *Overlay* (1983), feminist art historian Lucy Lippard bridged prehistoric and contemporary art by focusing on their corresponding needs to connect the sacred, the social and the environmental. In *Overlay*, Lippard describes how her one-year stay on a farm in Devon, in the south of England, precipitated a series of encounters with prehistoric art – megalithic sites, earth monuments, petroglyphs – that made her aware of the connection between the symbolic, environmental and social function of art, and its capacity to establish meaningful links between people, time and land. Without art, Lippard argues, 'culture remains simply one more manipulable commodity in a market society where even ideas and the deepest expressions of human emotion are absorbed and controlled'.[2]

Like Lippard, the three artists discussed in *Returning* found in the rural an environment propitious for the development of long-term initiatives that, utilising the methodologies and mindset of art – the tools provided by imagination, a form of radical questioning of anything given, the adoption of unique exploratory methods and formal outcomes – unfolded in ways that were socially and environmentally relevant. Their work gives value to and makes visible spaces and practices that are generally disregarded by mainstream institutional and commercial art contexts.

These practices focus on the local contexts within which these artists operate and which they often attempt to bridge with other sites of artistic and cultural production. Yet they are not simply shedding light on what lies in the *sidestream* (as opposed to the mainstream). With their displacement and activities, these artists question the neat, radical separation between the urban and the rural, the village and the city, the centre and the periphery, the static and the nomadic, as well as the identity of these realities as disconnected, polarised and stereotyped projections, the one shaped by tar and concrete, the other by peat and sheep. Here, the analysis of recent practices of *returning* to the land within the arts starts in the mid-2000s and continues beyond the publication of this book, as it acknowledges the expanded and more-than-human temporality that shapes the gestures of those who decide to return to the land, to revolve it and around it, and to synchronise themselves with its rhythms.

INLAND'S PEDAGOGY

Coming from a background in fine art and agroecology, the Madrid-born artist Fernando García-Dory (b.1978) joined the grassroots organisation Rural Platform, a movement of small farmers affiliated to La Via Campesina.[3] That was in 1998. A few years later, in 2005, García-Dory proposed the creation of a Commission for Rural Art within Rural Platform. This was an important call for the valorisation of the role that art can play in bringing attention to, channelling infrastructural support for and above all redefining the identity of the rural as a space that is charged with stereotypes, projections and misconceptions. García-Dory was initiating this call from his own experience and struggles. During the previous year, in 2004, he started planning a Shepherds' School, which officially launched in the Cantabrian Mountains of northern Spain in 2007 and remains active up to the present day.

Facing the issues of the territory where it started, the school began as a practical attempt to prevent the extinction

THE ARTIST AS ECOLOGIST

of pastoralist culture in northern Spain. For it, García-Dory recovered a family farm where in the 1970s his father had preserved ancient and local species of cows, amidst the push of the Green Revolution towards the introduction of high-yield breeds. The pedagogical and artistic project embraces a sense of the usefulness of art. Its school does not focus on the picturesque and contemplative aspects of countryside life. Instead, it consists of an intense study of specific disciplines, such as mountain topography and ecology, transhuman traditions, European livestock-rearing policies, veterinary and animal-rearing techniques, cheese-making know-how and shepherding history. Students learn in close contact with shepherd mentors and are exposed to months of training that teaches them how to herd, milk, slaughter and breed cows, sheep and goats in traditional ways.

Led by the artist, the Shepherds' School is conceived for the management of small to medium-sized herds. Its teaching embraces a critical and proactive perspective towards the modernisation of traditional practices. It updates and revises conventional knowledge, combining it with modern organic farming practices. Over its 20 years of existence, the curriculum of the Shepherds' School has expanded to incorporate such subjects as Landscape Management and Fire Prevention with Flocks (which relies on an economy of grazing and not of slaughtering or milking), Socio-environmental Services and Pastoralism, or Pastoralism and Gender.

Despite the school's dedication to the animals and care for the welfare of flocks, the coexistence of traditional pastoralism with the claims of animal-rights groups is still complex. The agendas, realities and socioeconomic needs of pastoralism don't entirely match current advances in animal consciousness and emotions that call for the recognition of animal rights, question human sovereignty over other species, and reflect on the impact of livestock rearing in terms of carbon emission and habitat transformation, particularly on a scale that is larger than the one addressed here. Similarly, the school seems to differentiate between those animals which ought to be protected (as they are, and produce, human assets) and those that threaten human organisation and economy, as when the artist expresses his reserve in relation to wolves: 'In the [19]80s the wolves moved in. As there are more than 2500 wolves in Spain it is not considered an endangered species. In the last 20 years wolf attacks have killed around 30% of the flocks in the mountains, with no control over their territorial scope or population.'[4]

It would be interesting to complement such revitalisation of pastoral traditions with a more humane pastoralist philosophy, in line with contemporary art's embrace of critical animal studies, in harmony with the animals (cattle and wildlife, but also wolves and other wild species), and beyond a polarising logic that divides animals into profitable and not-profitable and an extractivist logic that renders grazing bodies into goods. For this, a fundamental dialogue between scientists, ecologists and local communities should be further stimulated, so as to prevent the politicisation of viewpoints that privilege human goals over the rights of wildlife and livestock.

THE ARTIST AS AGROECOLOGIST

With the connection to Rural Platform evolving through various forms of collaboration, in 2007, while the Shepherds' School was taking its first steps, García-Dory published *The Artist as Agroecologist*, a manifesto in which he proposed a set of tools to 'preserve a living rural world' and where he launched the theoretical foundations for the development of his work. The concept of co-evolution is central to the manifesto, standing for a wisdom around the joint management of rural and wild biodiversity, as seen in the Portuguese *Montado* system, in which agrarian and natural, human and nonhuman communities co-evolved together. García-Dory's attempt to understand how artistic means can contribute to regenerating rural communities and the conscious production and distribution of food is valuable. Indeed, his theoretical, editorial and infrastructural work (all aspects of his artistic practice) have helped to bridge the questions and interests

THE ARTIST AS ECOLOGIST

of the institutional context of the arts with those of rural environments and small-scale agricultural systems.

These connections are relevant because they have the potential to regenerate the communitarian life that has often been lost in rural areas, one which activates long-lasting relationships between people and land, creating flows of ideas, goods and funding. While trying to find answers to how art may operate within what he calls an 'agroecological perspective', García-Dory proposes combining his own experience and artistic network with the knowledge and creativity of peasant reality, to generate forms of mutual learning and training aimed at devising systems of reciprocity and collective gain. It is from the initial proposal to create a Commission for Rural Art and the manifesto which followed that INLAND (a translation of the Spanish *Campo Adentro*) emerged in 2009 as a project about an agroecological and artistic para-institution. Described by García-Dory as a 'social sculpture and cultural strategy ... that examines the roles of territories, geopolitics, culture and identity between the city and the countryside', INLAND became an experimental platform for the exchange of situated knowledge and work methodologies between localised roots and national and international ramifications. Departing from the revitalisation of a village in the mountainous area of Asturias in the north of Spain, INLAND's aim has been, according to García-Dory, to 'try to create the countryside and art system I would like to live in'.[5]

INLAND'S PHASES

INLAND evolved in three phases. The first (2010–13) consisted of a real experiment in displacement, mobility and outreach. For this, the artist started by identifying 22 participating villages across Spain, each of which would host a resident artist for a given duration (which varied between two months and two years), where they would work on a specific case-study in association with Rural Platform. The artists, selected both through an open call and by direct invitation, stayed with a hosting farmer and received training at Rural Platform's headquarters in the requalified village of Amayuelas de Abajo, in the region of Castile and León.[6] This initial format allowed INLAND to test forms of intervention and familiarise the artists – who included among their number Mario García Torres, Can Altay, Emma Smith and the collective Wochenklausur – with non-rural practices and with their new contexts, and vice-versa. The residency was accompanied by the organisation of an international conference, exhibitions and presentations of the artistic outcomes, events that helped to stimulate the debate and connect diverse communities working on art and rurality in local, national and international contexts.

The second phase of INLAND (2013–15) was characterised by reflection and discussion. It was articulated through the launch of a series of encounter and study groups on art and rurality that were supported by Spanish and Dutch art institutions with a strong tradition of social engagement, namely Casco in Utrecht and Matadero in Madrid. The groups met to debate such topics as current theories associated to posthumanism and new environmentalist thinking (connected to critiques of anthropocentrism and acknowledging the impact of humankind on the planet); landscape theory (concerning different visions of how spaces are transformed, used and perceived); applied agroecology within a postcolonial framework (taking into account the entanglement of colonialism with the history of global food systems and conceiving ways in which agricultural and agrarian labour culture may be improved); and the economic and social conditions of art under post-Fordism (namely the impact of the atomisation, precarisation and fragmentation of labour relations on art production). To accompany and support the diffusion of the ideas that emerged from these encounters, INLAND published a series of *Field Notes*, booklets that focused on the themes covered and their relationship to ecology and food regenerative systems.

From 2016 onwards, INLAND entered its third phase, defining itself as 'a platform of land-based collaborations,

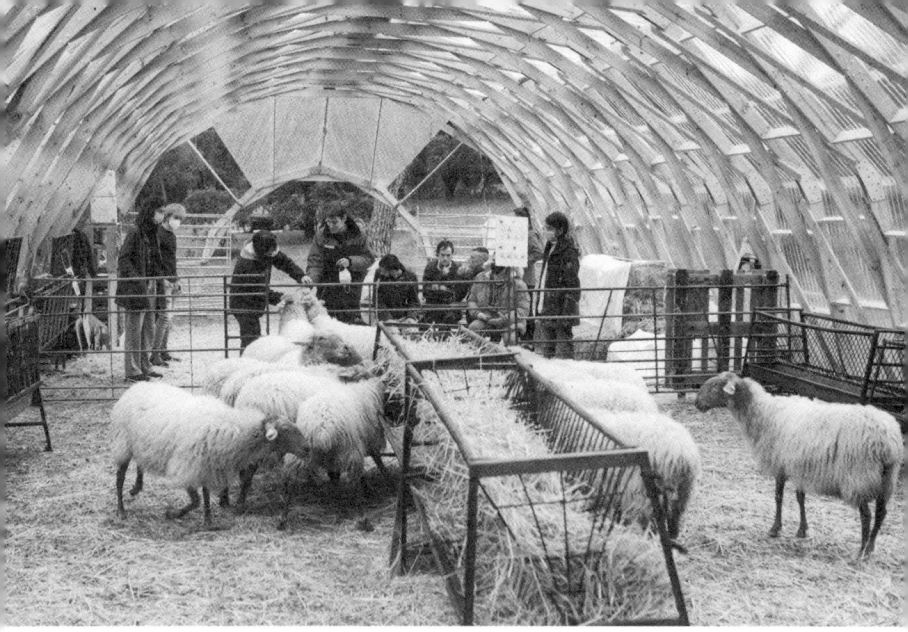

Fig.7   INLAND Rural Sheepfold. Production: Asociación Campo Adentro;
Plan design: Sergio Bravo / Campo Adentro

economies and communities-of-practice as a substrate for
post-Contemporary Art cultural forms'.[7] It currently operates
on various fronts, which range from the publication of books
and the participation in and organisation of exhibitions,
to the management of the Shepherds' School, the maintenance
of a flock of sheep in the Casa de Campo Park (fig.7), the largest
public park in Madrid (situating an agricultural practice at the
heart of a European capital) and the production and selling of
cheese. INLAND has also acted as a consultant for the European
Union Commission on the value of art for rural development
policies while facilitating and mobilising a grassroots pastoralist
movement, the European Shepherds Network – part of the
World Alliance of Mobile Indigenous Peoples and Pastoralists
which García-Dory cofounded in 2007.

The project creates opportunities for artists, farmers,
intellectuals, rural development agents, policymakers, writers
and curators to encounter one another and discuss each other's
needs and agendas, and to envisage ways of working together.

These encounters can happen in a remote village residency or in the context of an international exhibition. For instance, for Documenta 15 (2022), INLAND presented an 'un-folk museum' at Kassel's Museum of Natural History Ottoneum. It consisted of a conventional exhibition of objects and artworks where fragments of INLAND's visual and sound archives on pastoralism and forest ecology met with objects of rural culture and their descriptions. In parallel to the show, INLAND held a series of initiatives in Kassel, including sessions of their postgraduate annual programme INLAND Academy, a cheese-curing workshop and a Cheese Pavilion in which to sell it. Within the spirit of this particular edition of Documenta, the exhibition challenged the canon of art practice and presented copious initiatives whose social, political and relational missions were in dialogue with the aesthetics and discourses of art. While many of the activities were public, others were incompatible with many visitors' schedules or limited to the members of the collective.

This tension, between the communities engaged in imagining ways to create a better dialogue for a more sustainable world and the concrete possibilities for outreach and sharing allowed by the cultural infrastructures used to support them, challenged the logics of openness of such a large-scale cultural event and showed both the possibilities and the limitations of this kind of practice. Yet this seemed consistent with García-Dory's *modus operandi*, largely expressed through INLAND's own identity, scopes and functioning. A certain reliance on the organisation of closed-doors events, embraced as a means to prevent a genuine initiative from entering into a logic of spectacle and feeding the picturesque quest for authenticity within cultural tourism, is generally found in the artist's relationship with the Asturian village that INLAND is rehabilitating. This resistance to turn the activities of INLAND into a spectacle is perceptible, for instance, in the artist's refusal to provide its exact location to curators and art professionals, preventing potential visitors from touristifying and exoticising a place that, in its essence, is productive and imaginative but not performative.

In parallel, in his fight against the gentrification of the countryside, which he has described as a process of 'Disneyfication', the artist maintains that the arts in a rural context need to have a direct engagement with agriculture, with a 'radicality that gets to the roots', defying demands for rural tourism and branding which dispossess and strip rural workers of their concrete role in society. Instead, by moving away from spectacle, art helps to valorise the peasant identity and empower Indigenous and farming communities in their concrete capacity to manage land and life and in their sovereignty over the resources they foster.

FUTUREFARMERS' ASSEMBLAGES

Proposing the possibility of the rural existing as a mindset rather than a mere location, Californian artist and designer Amy Franceschini (b.1970) created Futurefarmers in 1995, a pioneering contemporary art collective for art and design connected to social practices. This title, which propels the gesture of returning towards the times to come, is connected to Franceschini's family history. Her mother was an organic food campaigner and her father a small-scale industrial farmer who fought for labour rights as vigorously as, paradoxically, he battled for the right to use chemical pesticides. Throughout its existence, Futurefarmers has continuously explored multidisciplinary approaches that combine scientific knowledge, experimental methodologies and social interactions and assemblages. These concern food knowledge, production and exchange, often taking place in urban environments, creating opportunities for people to come together. Its core group consists of Franceschini together with artists Michael Swaine, Marthe Van Dessel and Lode Vranken, who, according to the characteristics and needs of each project, may be joined by other people, experts with independent practices who have a common interest in experimentation, communal life and agricultural-related initiatives.

As happens with most experiments combining social practices, the territories in which they operate and those that traverse and constitute them, the activities of Futurefarmers resist description and categorisation, even though they are well documented in publications and on the group's website. Their nature as ongoing projects rather than as stable artworks, their complexity, the way they unfold into numerous, intangible experiences which mostly exist in the memories of those who took part in them, and the fact that they often make sense in relation to a set of projects and visions, make them hard to pin down and describe with certitude and objectivity. Futurefarmers operates through an accumulation of procedures and frameworks for exchange, all of which matter. Unlike an exhibition, which tends to result from a research or artistic project, many of these initiatives are messy, opaque and hard to categorise. They are the result of many steps by different agents, and of forms of immaterial transmission and temporal coherence that stimulate gatherings and rituals unfolding over time.

Despite such immateriality, the initiatives that Futurefarmers create provide important and direct contributions to the places and communities it collaborates with. Embedded with an artistic will and methodology, these projects activate relationships, shed light in situated forms of thinking and making and create long-lasting possibilities of togetherness that reassemble communities in places where they have been dismantled while creating modes of gathering that were previously non-existent. By departing from an artistic standpoint, Futurefarmers connects people and places through food production, preparation and consumption in ways that are not merely utilitarian or market-driven. This does not imply that art museums and galleries do not have such convening and community-building capacities. However, by often happening outside classical institutional frameworks, or by connecting an artistic context with other realms of society, Futurefarmers' initiatives have the potential to generate concrete, enduring experiments and explorations on forms of togetherness across people, lands and food systems.

THE ARTIST AS ECOLOGIST

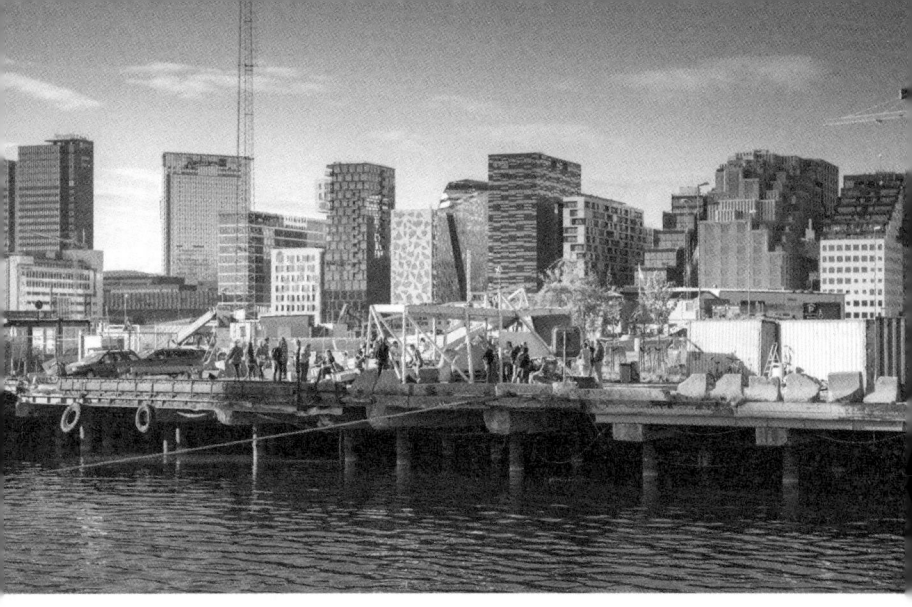

Fig.8   Futurefarmers, *Flatbread Society*, Temporary Bakehouse, Oslo, 2013.
Photograph by Max McClure

Flatbread Society

Many of these initiatives then gain an independent life and
unfold into unconventional partnerships that often reroute
art funding to local initiatives that contribute to generating
jobs and influence policymaking. They can assume the form
of publications, radio- and field-recording sessions, forms of
communal living, schools, shops or workshops. Such is the
case of one of Futurefarmers' longest projects, *Flatbread Society*
(fig.8), a permanent artwork initiated in 2012 in common land
on the waterfront redevelopment in the region of Bjørvika,
in Oslo's former container port. The Fjord City, as the whole
redevelopment scheme was called, was Oslo's largest urban
development scheme since the 17th century (when a fire in the
old town forced the displacement of the city centre). Its goal
was to free waterfront areas for private housing, commerce
and entertainment. Following an agenda of 'sustainable
development', the project aimed at generating a vital area
for the city, hosting symbolic bastions of the country's

culture and economy, including the National Opera House, the Munch Museum, the Deichmanske Library, the National Stock Exchange and the Norwegian headquarters of the multinational assurance firm PricewaterhouseCoopers. Given its large scale and the multiplicity of economic, social and political interests at stake, the Fjord City was widely debated in the Norwegian press and media, different visions conflicting with one another, including those that questioned and asserted the role that culture and art should play in such major urban plans with the tension between gentrification and revitalisation.[8]

Bjørvika Utvikling (the organisers of the cultural strategies for the Bjørvika waterside development), commissioned by and in collaboration with Anne Beate Hovind, an urban arts developer, invited Futurefarmers to conceive a project that would activate long-term social and community engagement in an area whose social and communal life was yet to be realised.[9] Together, Amy Franceschini, Stijn Schiffeleers, Lode Vranken and Marthe Van Dessel submitted a proposal to create a permanent public artwork that would stand for the solid tradition of agrarian land and knowledge sharing in Norway and would act as a unifying element across the area's local and migrant communities. They identified flatbread – a thin, crispy bread widely consumed in Norway – as a currency that circulates on a daily basis across populations and cultures of Oslo, proposing the creation of a multi-layered space for making and consuming it. *Flatbread Society* was conceived to facilitate the various steps needed to make the bread, from its inception in grain, whose use triggers, in Futurefarmers' words, 'a prismatic impetus to consider the interrelationship of food production to realms of knowledge sharing, cultural production, socio-political formations and everyday life',[10] to the tables and chairs where people sit and eat together.

In sharp contrast with the sleek, modern architecture that characterises much of the area, *Flatbread Society* materialises itself in an arable field dedicated to nine ancient grains, which were rescued from extinction and returned to the soil and whose existence was a symbol of the diversity that constituted

THE ARTIST AS ECOLOGIST

and thrived on this common land. Next to the field, there is a Bakehouse formed out of a skeletal wooden structure that resembles an inverted boat that is either being dismantled or repaired. The Bakehouse's architecture was inspired by a fleet of rescue boats from 1895, which were in the Oslo harbour and had been designed by Norwegian naval architect Colin Archer (1832–1921).[11] Connecting the notions of rescuing and returning, from the rescue boats that inspired the Bakehouse's architecture to the ancient grain seeds that were rescued and returned to the land, the collective honoured the possibilities of life re-emerging in cyclical forms, from the land to the sea and back.

Hosting three different bread ovens, the Bakehouse is complemented by DIY tables and benches in wood, a community radio station (Radio Ramona) that gives voice to the project, and a shelter structure. Adjacent to the urban farm, next to the Oslo fjord and surrounded by Bjørvika's modern buildings, the Bakehouse, with its experimental architecture, has a paradoxical existence that encapsulates many of the efforts and limitations of those who try to merge the spirit of urban development and rural cultures. It stands for the clash between the ideology of common land versus the private property development and ownership of the apartments and office buildings that characterise the new urban planning for the area. While demonstrating that alternative, more sustainable and gentle ways of building and living are possible, the Bakehouse operates in a dynamic of permanent friction and resistance. Its own existence challenges the logic of spatial occupation and the culture of privatised public space that the whole regenerated area stands for and, while giving it a soul, it is inevitably tokenised.

Yet it is exactly in this dysfunctionality that Futurefarmers ascribe the significance of the initiative: 'The starting point for Bakehouse should not be a place of critical agitation, but rather a "strange" place where convictions disappear because it is such a strange place. This is where the arts come in: the magic and the amazement that stops the discussion and starts the dialogue in a Socratic dialectic manner.'[12] In being this bizarre, out of place entity that is aligned with the temporalities of grain preparation and baking, and also connected to the rediscovery and circulation of ancient, non-industrialised cereals and grains, the Bakehouse becomes a capsule in time and space, from which the individuals who use it and the communities that gather around it can remember one of the most ancestral histories of human food preparation while configuring its renewed possibilities in the present-future times of changing paradigms and ecosystems.

AS ABOVE, SO BELOW

When considering community gatherings around ancestral rituals that evoke the magic of everyday life concerning food and nature, it is important to consider those artists who have chosen to embrace spirituality and holistic practices to activate synergies and create mindful relationships between individuals and the natural environment. Again, this is not a new strategy. Critics like Lucy Lippard, in her previously mentioned book *Overlay*, sought to analyse the desire of artists to search for and create modes of ritualistic connection between bodies, the divine and the land. While those attempts were often driven by the desire to reassess art's relevance in a society that was undergoing a quick process of transformation and modernisation, the artists who are seeking spiritual and ecological consistency during the first decades of the 21st century seem to be searching for a healing of the self and a connection between the individual and both the cosmic and the earthly worlds. The expression 'as above, so below', originally extracted from the ancient occultist text the *Emerald Tablet*, has been adopted by many artists to express their desire to shed light on the interconnectedness of all life and harmonise the relationship between the macro and the micro-cosmos, the celestial and the earthly, the microbial and the planetary.[13]

Embracing such a connection between the organic, the technological and the mystic, French-Guianese-Danish artist Tabita Rezaire (b.1989) adopts a practice of chanting and enchanting, which emerges from her interest in eco-spirituality and is currently rooted on Amakaba, a women-led agro-ecological cacao farm and spiritual retreat that she founded in French Guiana. As she describes it:

> I sing in remembrance of a time-space where data flows from the 'cosmos database' to our inner information portals. I sing in defiance to restore our lineage of scientific knowledge ... By engaging with African and Indigenous ancestral technologies of information and communication, we dare to reconcile the worlds of organic matter, energy and electronics to nurture a mystic-techno-consciousness. So we sing to decolonise and heal our technologies.[14]

Following these aims, much of Rezaire's early work combined a mid-2000s post-internet aesthetics with a feminist, post-colonial agenda and a growing interest in the activation of ritualistic explorations.

The video installation *Mamelles Ancestrales* (2019), one of the last works she made before concentrating her efforts in Amakaba, denotes a syncretism in which these varied interests were brought together. Inspired by the Senegambian megalithic stone circles, the artist created a stone circle installation composed of 12 large stones, accompanied by a 60-minute video, presented on a monitor on the ground at its centre. In the video, the artist explores her interest in these ancient megaliths due to their astronomical alignment and connection between the sky and the Earth. She also makes a call for a 'decolonial archaeology', while claiming back the land and traditions that hosted the original stones (the video was shot in four African megalithic sites: Sine Ngayène and Wanar in Senegal and Wassu and Kerbatch in Gambia). While questioning the supremacy of scientific and academic knowledge over spiritual and popular experience, which she classifies as an inheritance of a dominant colonial mindset, Rezaire moves beyond representation and symbolism, working on site and documenting the experiences of those who inhabit this land, a step that heralded the life-changing adventure she was about to initiate the following year.

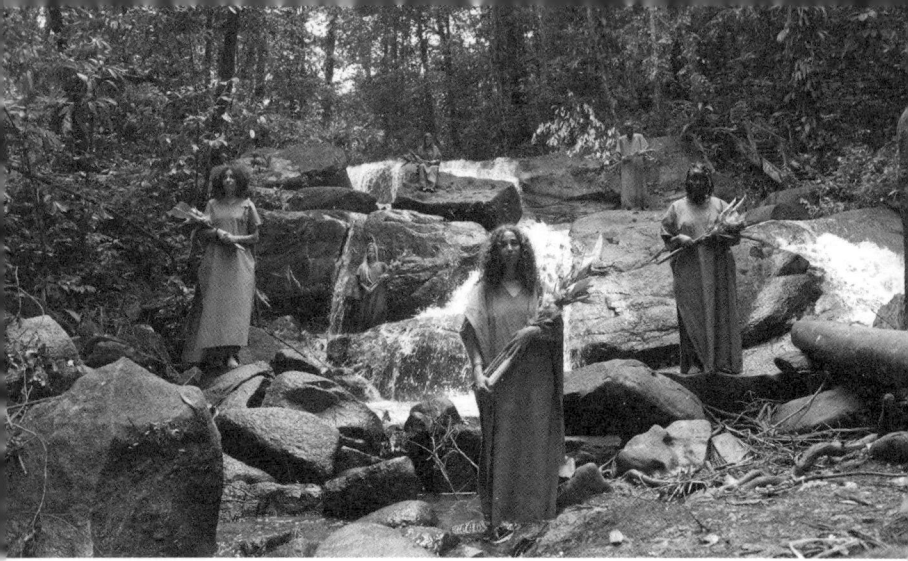

Fig.9   Amakaba team during a ceremony in the Amazonian forest
of French Guiana, where the initiative is based, 2021

AMAKABA

Amakaba started in 2020, when Rezaire exchanged her birth
town of Paris for Mount Mahury, a coastal massif south
of Cayenne, in her father's home country of French Guiana
(fig.9). A word coined by Rezaire, Amakaba is, for her, 'a place
of gathering between people, land, insects, ancestors, and
spirits in the heart of the Amazon forest in French Guiana.
A place of transmission for the wisdom of the earth, the body,
and the cosmos.'[15] A healing and knowledge centre, Amakaba
merges Rezaire's interests in art, science, feminism and
spirituality with her mission to establish a cacao agroecological
farm together with a kundalini yoga and meditation centre.
It is a substantial challenge, to implement a model of gentle
agroforestry (which consists of the coexistence of trees and
other naturally occurring vegetation in a non-invasive farming
system that balances environmental, economic and social
benefits) in a territory such as the Amazon, so drastically
scarred by industrial-scale agrobusiness. Even more to do so
with an artistic and creative mindset interested in questioning

not only where and when art happens but also why and how art can contribute to environmental and societal change.

Being a women-led initiative that merges agrarian science and a spiritual mission, Amakaba supports Rezaire's investment in challenging dominant Western powers and patriarchal logics of access to resources, knowledge and labour. As will be discussed further, this goal is aligned with her interest in using digital technologies to recuperate and bring to light expressions of ancestral, non-Western knowledge (as when she documented the medicinal and herbal experience of French-Guianese doulas in the 2022 video *L'art de naître*). As such, Rezaire creates instruments for the survival and transmission of experiences that might otherwise be lost, while contributing to the recognition and emancipation of local communities of women and the strengthening of their identity, role and relationship to the land. Beyond being a production hub, Amakaba also becomes an open space for local women to assemble, exchange ideas and knowledge, and collaborate with one another and with guests.

At the same time, Rezaire's consolidated artistic reputation allowed her to attract attention and funding to her project. Insisting that Amakaba is a place with a specific agenda and set of relations and not a commodifiable artwork, the artist largely engages herself with art commissions and exhibitions that can support Amakaba logistically or economically. For instance, during a 2022 interview, she stated that 'Now I'm looking for a museum to buy us chocolate machines. If anyone is reading this, reach out.'[16]

Such interest is also reciprocal. In 2022, for *Persons Persones*, the 8th Biennale Gherdëina, in the Italian Alps, Rezaire agreed to present a video installation in exchange for a fee donated to Amakaba. The work shown, the above-mentioned *L'art de naître*, revisits the 'personhood' theme of the Biennale through the lens of the divine feminine and its role in the creation of life. *L'art de naître* documents the knowledge and experience of four French-Guianese doulas who, from their respective ethnic and cultural backgrounds, supported and cared for the inception of motherhood: Mrs Yapara, from the Indigenous Lokono tradition; Odette and Noria Majokko, from the Maroon Saramaka tradition; and Mrs Myriam Kerrel from the Creole tradition. The recollections, anecdotes and know-how of these women disclose, in a way which is practical, technical and spiritual, some of the core concerns of Amakaba's mission and the artist's own journey as a doula of human and more-than-human life. Following in the footsteps of her grandmother and great-grandmother, both midwives, Rezaire is now birthing the many lives that, in the Guianese forest, are coming out of her desire to connect and heal the land, the people and the environment that hosts them, in spirit and matter. As such, she demonstrates how, even in the Amazonian forest, a different rural is possible: a rural that is not new, nor static, nor disappearing.

García-Dory, Futurefarmers and Rezaire, the three artists discussed in *Returning*, share this emphasis on imagining and building a future that isn't necessarily dictated by the logics and rhythms of production, circulation and consumption – of land, food and cultural products alike – of the late capitalist industrialised society. Through their activities, alongside those that join them, they demonstrate art's fundamental role in proposing slower, more caring, more balanced and still efficient ways of relating to the land and the soil. Their work connects people and the various entities – animal, vegetal, mineral – that are essential in agricultural contexts. It proposes consistent experiences of togetherness shaped by creative and participatory methodologies. By reinventing methods and relationships, it breaks with the nostalgic aura that the countryside still holds.

If their biggest challenge is to imagine sustainable, vivid and concrete forms of merging the spaces of rural production with those of presentation associated with contemporary art, the fact that these artists are not making work about their condition and experience but making food or creating spaces through art signals a radical shift from any forms of depiction and representation of pastoral, bucolic environments. The practical ways in which they call for more consistent, sustainable and

　　　　　THE ARTIST AS ECOLOGIST

caring ways of connecting people and the land, and of establishing forms of lasting alliances that reinforce existing and build new communities where there were none, are essential in today's world, given the connection between environmental devastation and global food-production necessities.

By promoting the revitalisation of desertified rural areas, as in the case of INLAND; creating new communities concentrated around the production of bread from the land to the table, as with Futurefarmers' *Flatbread Society*; or establishing an experimental sanctuary in which the forest and the mind are cared for through an ecofeminist, decolonial approach, as in Rezaire's centre for the arts and science of the earth, Amakaba, these artists offer concrete examples of balanced food and land-healing procedures. As such, they validate the importance of art in society, not merely as a system of illustrating and communicating harm and beauty but first and foremost as a method of proposing other ways of living and consuming. Their procedures and practices are based around activities that are much more than symbolic and metaphorical. The rootedness and materiality of their work demonstrates that other ways of farming, eating and living are viable.

These calls for acting beyond representation will be further discussed in the following chapter, *Performing*, which investigates artistic expressions that bypass forms of representation of climate breakdown to instead express a somatic, corporeal reality with a concrete, affective strength. The chapter focuses on case-studies that take place both within and outside the institutional framework of the museum and art gallery. It stands in between the decisions to embrace land operations analysed in *Returning* and those that revise and reconceptualise the possibilities and formats of the presentation of artworks which will be later considered in *Reverberating* and *Exhibiting*.

Chapter 3

Performing

If *Returning* addressed the ways in which artists have chosen to work with and for the land, and how these choices have shaped their relationship to the institutional frameworks of contemporary art, *Performing* comments on the openness of contemporary art towards live and time-based media and its engagement with environmental concerns. It discusses how artistic production that addresses ecology intersects with the fields of performance and dance, which since the 2010s have been integrated within art exhibitions in the institutional, independent and commercial realms, as well as in diverse events, such as festivals, art fairs or symposia. This interest of contemporary art in live events did not escape the notice of those working across performative media, from dancers and choreographers to those engaged with experimental traditions of theatre. As early as 2011, choreographer Mårten Spångberg noted that 'the entire visual art world has developed obsessive-compulsive relations to dance. MoMA just engaged a research team to explore options to incorporate performance in the collection, and mind you there isn't a biennale that has forgotten to emphasize the importance of performance elements.'[1]

With nuances, this interest persists. Beyond the merging of disciplines, performance acts often incorporate forms of creation which derive from the lived and experienced present. As such, and reflecting the widespread growth of environmental preoccupations, artists have also employed live media, namely performance, to express their concerns in ways that are dynamic, direct and that propose different ways of being and acting upon the world. Movement research seems particularly suitable to address these concerns, as it allows creators, practitioners and audiences to imagine, rehearse and experiment with how bodies may exist and act differently. By departing from concrete somatic changes, these proposals bring hope that the repair of trouble, as well as its grief and acceptance, may be achievable through the transformation of how people relate to their bodies and to one another.

BEYOND REPRESENTATION

The artworks discussed here are not symbolic acts of healing and togetherness, which, despite abounding in the arts' context, are for the most part metaphoric, acting as a sort of placebo palliative care and inducing the perception of benefit rather than actual physiological effects. Going beyond the mere ritualistic, the works of artists Joan Jonas; Rugilė Barzdžiukaitė, Vaiva Grainytė and Lina Lapelytė; and Eduardo Navarro, which are the focus of this chapter, trigger an investigation on the limits and possibilities of what can be enacted and shared beyond representation and illustration. They offer meaningful case-studies for the ways in which *performing* can contribute to an environmentally relevant reconceptualisation of life.

During a workshop for professional and amateur dancers entitled *The Climate The Worry The Dance*, which Spångberg led in 2022, the choreographer acknowledged that 'in order to save the world, the Earth and / or the planet, it's not nature that we need to preserve ... as long as our mentalities towards the world, at a micro- or macro-level, are upheld, all those efforts and endless amounts of money will only save us, at the best, for an extra 20 minutes.'[2] While the potential limits of art, dance and performance's engagement with ecology are clear, as the results may simply mirror what is happening and is already widely known to most people, the ways to bring about actual change through artistic creation are harder to pin down. Three recent attempts to go beyond representation, to bypass critique and to activate changes in bodies and mindsets are discussed here.

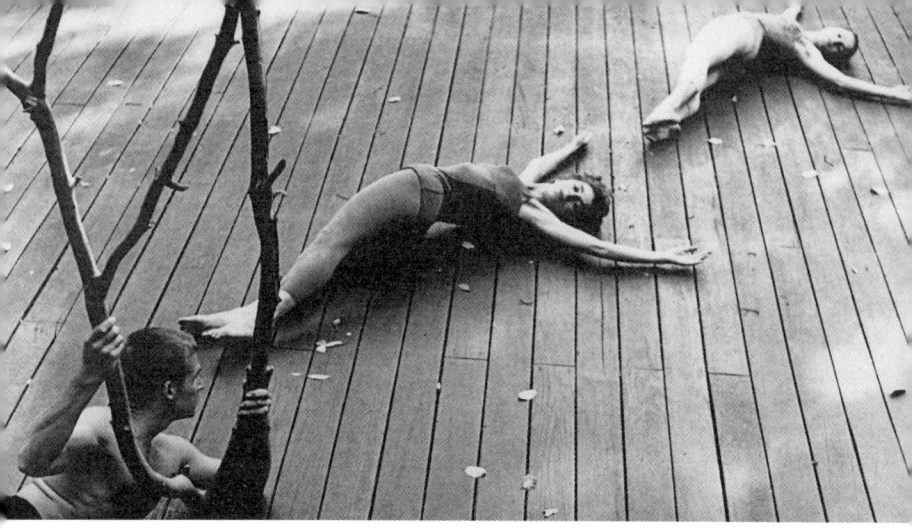

Fig.10   Anna Halprin, A.A. Leath and Simone Forti in Anna Halprin's
The Branch. Photograph taken at the Halprin Dance Deck, Kentfield, CA, *c.*1957

   Yet, as observed in the other chapters, the existence of environmental concerns within movement and performance is not new. For instance, while exploring the possibilities of connecting human and vegetal movement, in 1960 the pioneer choreographer and dancer Anna Halprin (1920–2021) declared: 'my concern is form in nature – like the structure of a plant – not in its outer appearance, but in its internal growth process'.[3] From the mid-1950s onwards, Halprin led her teaching at her open-air deck on Mount Tamalpais, near Kentfield in northern California. The deck had been built by her husband, architect Lawrence Halprin, an alumnus of Bauhaus professors Walter Gropius and Marcel Brauer.[4] Located in the redwood forest that still today surrounds her house, the platform incorporates the trees, which become active presences as they emerge from holes on the floor, as in *The Branch*, which Halprin performed on the deck at the end of the 1950s together with Simone Forti and A.A. Leath (fig.10). Halprin's deck contributed to the non-urban expansion of the sites where Western dance was taking place. It also played an important role in the production and reception of dance in tune with the natural environment.

During the same period, artist Simone Forti (b.1935), one of Halprin's students, created an iconic artwork that questioned the human and animal monopoly of movement. *Onion Walk* or *Onion on a Glass Bottle* (1961) is a sculptural and choreographic piece that recognises the agency of movement of an onion, surprising viewers while inviting them to go beyond the anthropocentric temporality of performance observation. As Forti described, 'An onion which had begun to sprout was set on its side on the mouth of a bottle. As the days passed it transferred more and more of its matter from the bulb to the green part, until it had so shifted its weight that it fell off.'[5] What could be seen as a conceptual exercise was actually an important step towards a de-anthropomorphising of performance and dance. With this gesture, rather than critiquing a faulty system, illustrating the gloom of a world in crisis (a consciousness that was already in the air at the time, as demonstrated by Rachel Carson's book *Silent Spring*, published in the US in 1962), or acting on behalf of a nonhuman, Forti offered the possibility of dance bypassing its cultural construction and incorporating the movement of nonhuman life.

JOAN JONAS: THE EVERYDAY AND THE MYTHICAL

Decades later, Joan Jonas (b.1936), who in her youth collaborated with Forti, combined these and other early modes of recognising the agency of nature with current concerns for a world in crisis. For over 50 years, Jonas has demonstrated a disciplinary elasticity rare in contemporary art, expressed through her performances (often involving her own presence, alone or in the company of others), drawings (many of animals), sculptures (often with abstract, geometric references), environments and video installations (which comprise all the above, as well as objects, props and complex display systems). More recently, her concerns about the environmental crisis and her interest in animal wellbeing became more evident in her work. They became particularly visible in 2013, when she created *they came to us without a word*, an installation of about a hundred large drawings of fish that responds to the decrease in global fish populations. Made for the CCA Kitakyushu Project Gallery in Japan, Jonas's work portrays each fish as an individual, with distinct features, and the drawings also attest to her outstanding skill at representing animals. The fragility and flimsiness of the paper sheets on which each fish is painted also express the animals' vulnerability. Presented as a large school of fish composed of three parallel rows of fish drawings – sequences of single fish painted in cobalt blue ink on white sheets of paper, suspended on strips by metallic binder clips – the assemblage emanated a poetic aura that mourned and grieved the depletion of the seas.

After Kitakyushu, Jonas continued merging the concrete and the figurative, the everyday and the mythical, in artworks that, in their unique way, portray animal-human co-dependencies and make visible the vulnerability of life. In 2016, the artist was invited to take part in a gathering of artists and thinkers organised by the TBA21–Academy, an art and environmental advocacy organisation focused on ocean preservation. The encounter was held during that year's Kochi-Muziris Biennale, in Kerala, India, where Jonas presented the performance *Kochi Oceans – sketches and notes* in a square adjacent to the Chinese fishing nets of Fort Kochi, traditional shore-operated lift nets that acted as a visible example of human relation to the extraction of resources from the sea. Jonas, assisted by artist Thao Nguyen Phan (b.1987), took the audience through a narrative of past and present wonders and troubles of the oceans. Bringing together sources and references, the performance combined readings of Herman Melville's novel *Moby Dick* (1851) and Italo Calvino's story *The Aquatic Uncle* (1963–4) with the live drawing of fishes – painted in blue tones, like those of Kitakyushu.

In the background, a large video projection combined fragments of 20th-century cinematographer Jean Painlevé's underwater films with footage of marine life shot by the artist in aquaria: fish, jellyfish, seals and starfish. A small bell dangling from each hand, Jonas wore delicate white clothes and, at moments, a paper mask covering her face. Acting between the projector and the images projected, close to the audience, her slender body moved with uncertain, uneven paces on the stage, followed by her own shadow, cast onto the projected images and doubling her theatrical persona. At times, she used the large sheets of paper on which she was drawing as a form of trap, placing them between the projector and the screen to capture the projected images of the animals on them, disclosing their condition of being prey. She exposed her own ageing, fragile body – human-turned-screen – absorbing the projected beings cast across it, and forming hybrid animal images with her; the endangered condition of the marine animals, the uncertainty of their lives, their use of a language beyond verbal expression, were all made visible by and through the artist's being. Jonas became the ocean – the words, fables and narratives that shape its imaginary, as well as the projections and realities that constitute it, along with the problems, disasters and hopes that inform multiple attempts at ecological struggle.

Moving Off the Land II

Emerging from *Kochi Oceans – sketches and notes*, Jonas's *Moving Off the Land II* is a multi-layered project that evolved over three years (fig.11). For it, Jonas assembled literary, folk and scientific texts about the oceans; visited, filmed and interacted with specialist staff in aquaria in the US and Japan; and collected historical, scientific and amateur footage of maritime and underwater scenes. She combined this with her own filmed material, including footage shot at TBA21's affiliated organisation, Alligator Head Foundation, dedicated to the preservation of maritime fauna and located in Jamaica, where she interviewed local fishermen and recorded short performances for the camera. Retitled as *Moving Off the Land II*, the work was presented at Tate Modern, London (2018), TBA21–Academy's Ocean Space in Venice, Italy (2019) and the Prado Museum in Madrid (2020).[6]

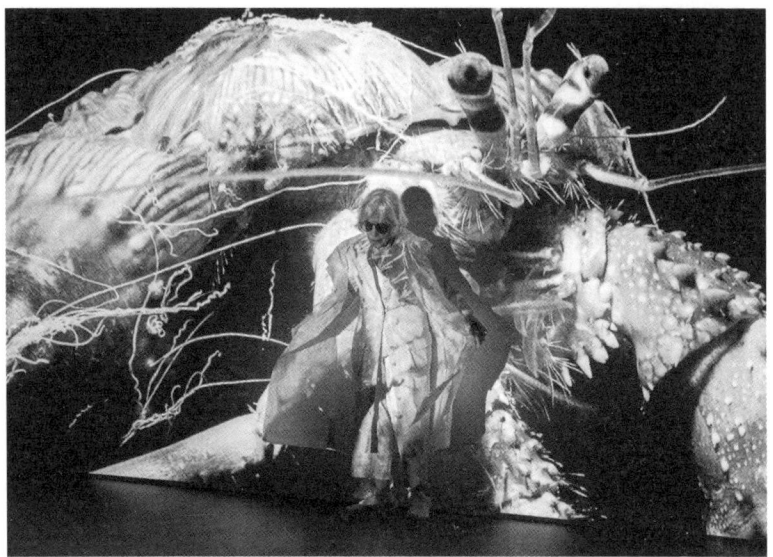

Fig.11   Joan Jonas, *Moving Off the Land II*, 2019, Ocean Space,
Chiesa di San Lorenzo, Venice. Performance with Ikue Mori and Francesco
Migliaccio. Commissioned by TBA21–Academy. Photograph by Moira Ricci

In a speech that marks the start of the performance,
Jonas dedicates the work to Rachel Carson, whose writing
is extensively featured in the work. She starts by reading an
extract from the American ecologist's book *The Edge of the Sea*
(1955), which describes the symbiotic lives of shrimp and other
sea creatures with sponges, underwater providers of life, food
and shelter. Music and other sound elements can be heard
throughout the event. At the beginning of the reading, melodic
chimes create an immersive environment, reinforced by the
absence of any light source besides the projection screen, which
leaves the artist, her collaborators and the objects on stage
in quasi-darkness. The dreamlike, slightly unreal atmosphere
induced by the chimes and the dim light are reinforced by
a video sequence of the artist's shadow walking towards the
water and wearing a wig of algae, before plunging into the sea.

'The mind evolved in the sea. Water made it possible ...
When animals crawled onto dry land, they took the sea with

THE ARTIST AS ECOLOGIST

them', Jonas read, quoting from philosopher of science Peter Godfrey-Smith's book *Other Minds: The Octopus, the Sea, and the Deep Origins of Consciousness* (2016). Throughout the work, the artist and the real and magical animals featured in it met in a site of fluidity, experimentation and loss of control. They co-existed across land and sea, real and magical, expressing their present-day challenges. Their joint presence disrupted the conventional structure of narrative (diluting beginning and end) and altered the sense of the passing of time. Together, they took viewers into a hypnagogic state.

AGENCY

Several scenes of *Moving Off the Land II* show animals in glass tanks and aquaria. A particularly compelling moment happens when a beluga whale is seen interacting with a small child, both trying to cross the pane that separates them and access a haptic experience that can never be fulfilled – for the glass that allows them to meet also prevents them from concretely touching one other. The white animal looks like its own ghost, a memory of its free counterparts. To observe this and other captive animals (in particular those behind reflective surfaces such as glass tanks and aquaria) is to accept seeing (but also to ignore) the human shadow cast upon them and to understand this shadow not as a mere reflection but as a perceptual constraint. The glass is at once protection, display and a material division that accentuates the separation between nature and culture. In parallel, the performance's projection screen acts as another membrane that separates whale and visitors and establishes a distinction between an active and a passive engagement with the animal and the apparatus that makes it accessible. The projection reinforces the distinction between the act of being close to the animal and the act of watching its video mediation.

But here, unlike Forti's *Onion Walk* and despite providing the subject and matter of the footage, the whale has little agency. Locked inside an aquarium, the animal must perform for spectators and camera and be unknowingly transposed to another kind of stage, where its images are projected as yet another version of the exhibitionary and theatrical event it has to permanently fulfil.[7] In this sense, it is not simply the violence of captivity and forceful entertainment that Jonas is bringing to light but also the violence inherent in the illicit transposition of an animal: with her artistic gesture, the artist replicates the aquarium's function, a framing and displacement of the animal that reinforces its captivity and its gradual death by exposure. Following this scene, Jonas shares the impressions of a marine biologist concerning the intelligence and sentience of large marine vertebrates, which accentuates the tension of the images previously presented. At the same time, she is drawing large sea animals, establishing a difference in tone and genre between the creatures projected and those she depicts: some real and captive, others imagined and free.

When analysing her involvement with the interlinking feminist discourse of the 1970s, Jonas explained how 'All of my work from maybe 1970 on referred to the feminist movement, but indirectly ... I wasn't interested in making political art, but from the very beginning I've always been interested in how my work relates to the present situation.'[8] In 2019, when invited to speak about her work's implications for ecology, Jonas declared: 'In recent years, the environmental situation has become more and more important to me and visible in my work, due to the increasing threats to our livelihoods and that of numerous other species'.[9] This parallelism between Jonas's oblique but important engagement with feminism during the 1970s and her commitment to ecology from the 2010s onwards – two pressing struggles that characterise each moment respectively – helps to position and elucidate her stance in *Moving Off the Land II*. Pursuing an investigation similar to that around the role women played as symbolic, spiritual, mystical figures in history and culture, which Jonas expressed through her art, the artist sets out to search for 'the role the ocean has played for cultures throughout history as a totemic, spiritual, and ecological touchstone'.[10]

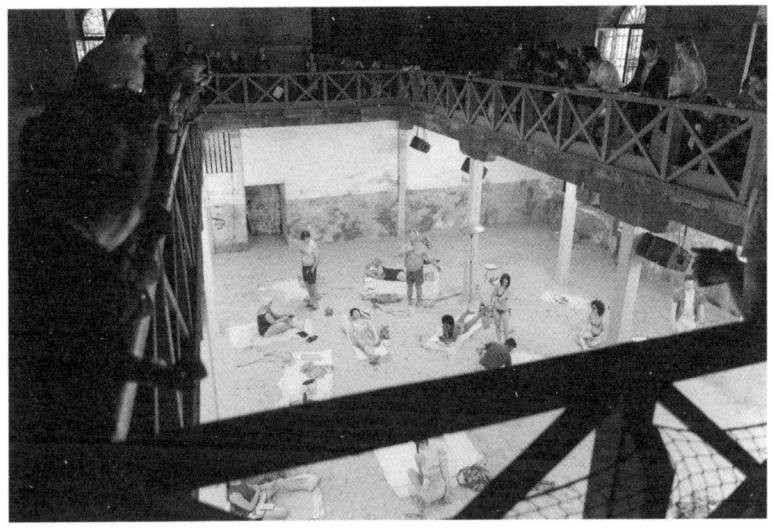

Fig.12 *Sun & Sea (Marina)*, opera-performance by Rugilė Barzdžiukaitė, Vaiva Grainytė and Lina Lapelytė at 58th Biennale Arte 2019, Venice. Photograph by Andrej Vasilenko

Sun & Sea's Holiday Choir

Moving from the ocean of Jonas's work to the seashore, *Sun & Sea (Marina)* is an opera-performance by Rugilė Barzdžiukaitė (b.1983), Vaiva Grainytė (b.1984) and Lina Lapelytė (b.1984) which was staged for the Lithuanian Pavilion at the 58th Venice Biennale in 2019, winning the artists the Golden Lion award for the best national pavilion. The work dwells on the contradictions of climate change in a spectacular manner, combining music and performance in a highly staged environment (fig.12). It combines the skills of the three artists – Barzdžiukaitė has a background in theatre, Grainytė is a writer and Lapelytė works in composition and performance – with the experience of conceiving live events of its curator, Lucia Pietroiusti, at the time Head of Ecologies at Serpentine, London.

This was the second collaboration between the three artists, following the opera *Have a Good Day!* (2011), which was also well received and which won a series of awards.[11] Defined by the artists as an opera-performance, the *mise en scène* for *Sun & Sea* is a beach where 17 singers and other cast members perform for roughly one hour. The work was first shown at the National Gallery of Art in Vilnius in 2017. In Venice, it was set in a 17th-century building of the Venetian Navy in the Arsenale area, close to the Biennale's central exhibitions. Accessing the show from a balcony that surrounded the stage below, audiences would watch, from above, a group of performers wearing summer clothes, swimsuits and sunglasses while pursuing everyday holiday activities: reading, sunbathing, eating a sandwich or playing with an inflatable ball. The scene resembled a conventional beach day, and almost nothing disrupted its tranquillity. The bright and pastel tones of the performers' clothes and props, the melodic jingles and voices of the singers, and the unremarkable intensity at which the whole scene unfolded were reassuringly familiar.

Sung to soft tunes derived from the tradition of musical theatre, the opera-performance's lyrics speak of personal and environmental events. Yet they are never joyful. Aspirations, idiocies, malaise and complaints abound: a wealthy woman wants her child to visit all the world's oceans, a widow explains how her ex-husband drowned while suffering a cramp due to magnesium insufficiency, a young man travelled to Portugal to watch a bullfight 'just for fun', a long-distance couple regret their next separation, a man reveals he has 'a tumour the size of an egg', while another woman protests about litter on the beach. No one seems happy or relaxed during their holidays, a feeling that may be familiar to many.

Several characters appear more than once: the workaholic, the wealthy mother or the complaining woman, intersected by the choir, which brings everyone's voices together, further accentuating their laments. The tension between the miseries of everyday life, as told in *Workaholic's Song* – 'I really don't feel that I can let myself slow down / Because my colleagues will look down at me / They'll see I have no strength of will / And I'll become a loser in my own eyes / Exhaustion, exhaustion, exhaustion, exhaustion …' – and a collapsing planet, as in

THE ARTIST AS ECOLOGIST

Song of Complaint – 'Everything is out of joint / The beginning of May brought frost and snow / And winter gives us buds and mushrooms' – makes evident the coexistence of normalisation and anxiety that dominates the existence of many people living under climate breakdown. This push and pull between consciousness and paralysis, awareness and impotence, and even horror and fascination is also entangled in another ironic song, *Chanson of Admiration* – 'Jellyfish dance along in pairs / With emerald-coloured bags / Bottles and red bottle-caps / Oh the sea never had so much colour'.

FAMILIAR STORIES

The most pertinent aspect of *Sun & Sea*, however, is not the characters' complaints about travel disruptions or personal health problems, or even the satirical portrayal of individual lives affected by the small events of climate breakdown. Rather, audiences have the possibility of recognising themselves in the situation, in what the singers recount but also in the theatrical setting where the piece takes place. This allows for the touristic style and spectacle that *Sun & Sea* makes use of – a mode of cultural consumption well established in our society – to be considered for its environmental implications. Neither conventional artwork, nor classical opera nor concert, *Sun & Sea* zigzags across different genres and formats, resisting the total immersion of spectators – the well-worn suspension of disbelief – always calling for a form of mediation. In Venice, as well as in several other places where the show has been presented, audiences viewed the beach from a bird's-eye view, creating a different level of engagement than if they were seated in a theatre or a concert hall, watching the show in front of them. They could move around the balcony but not access the space of the performance.

This tension between immersion and control, distance and closeness, adds a layer of complexity to the performance, for what is at stake is not merely the relationship between the calm beach setting and the chants of announced climate disaster.

With its theatrical apparatus, *Sun & Sea* asks audiences where they stand in relation to what they observe – at what level of empathy, sympathy or criticism do they engage with the re-creation of the beach and summer travels, with the singers' stories and complaints? How does the audience participate in this spectacle? Feelings might range from detachment to complicity, ridicule or fascination. By moving around, viewers can also decide their position in relation to the scene. They can opt to have a viewpoint that excludes any infrastructure or stage elements, which awakens their suspension of disbelief. Other viewers instead may opt to look at the hidden cables of the electric blankets, used to keep the singers warm in Venice during the chilly and humid May of 2019, which discreetly emerge in areas where the sand is thinner, thereby consciously reflecting on the tons of sand extracted from somewhere, the bright lamps that reproduce summer sunlight indoors, the emergency-exit doors and signs, and all the other logistical infrastructure employed to make this fiction verisimilar.

All this makes it clear that the carbon footprint of each theatre, art space or rented venue where *Sun & Sea* was exhibited is likely very high, reflecting, with humour and melancholy, the climate issues that the performers sing about. Accepting this reality, the artists and production team replicate the singers' voices by embracing the contradictions that surround climate awareness and activism. They throw the inflatable beach ball at members of the audience, asking them where they stand in all this, while making them aware that it is their own shadows, more than those of any hypothetical seagulls, that are cast upon the white sand, since without them, *Sun & Sea* would cease its globetrotting journey.

EDUARDO NAVARRO'S F.O.C.A

Working on actual shores, locally, and embracing performance as a therapeutic procedure for more-than-humans, since the COVID-19 lockdown artist Eduardo Navarro (b.1979) has been developing a project that, starting in an informal way, has been gradually structured into an initiative for the support of the welfare of marine animals. This direct engagement with animal life is a rather surprising twist in Navarro's practice. Like Jonas, he works across different media, which range from large-scale sculptures to wall pieces, drawings, performances, collective live actions and participatory installations. Through his work, Navarro has pursued ongoing questions that concern the functioning of the mind and its connection to nature and the cosmos. Interested in the ways perception mediates reality through the senses, he has often created environments and sensory experiences that activate the physical senses – taste, hearing, sight, smell and touch – and induce new, embodied ways of relating to art and of connecting to the world. These experiences have an important temporal dimension, as they require those who engage with them (and the artist) to go beyond the conventional observation of an artwork and enter a different mindset, closer to a meditative state. As Navarro describes it,

> I see the works as ways of contemplating. Contemplation and meditation have a lot in common. I try to make the audience contemplate something for a period of time that's really absurd, and at the same time they have to get rid of their preconceptions of what they're observing. Either you get into the mood of the work, which is a very slow process, or you see it for one second and you leave.[12]

Such is the case with *Vegetal Ear* (2021), a site-specific sculpture permanently installed in an eco-park near Guatemala City. Located in a broadleaf forest, the sculpture consists of a huge, plant-like form, whose interior visitors can access through a small door at the bottom that leads to a round, windowless chamber. This chamber is connected to a tall tube that terminates in a red flower with three yellow pistils that collect rainwater, from which birds may drink, and which connect the sounds of the exterior with its interior. In this dark, protected atmosphere, visitors can rest and sense the world beyond sight, as a plant.

The changes of rhythm brought about by the COVID-19 pandemic allowed Navarro to pursue his interest in the perceptive and expressive modes of other beings, and to further understand how art can have a positive impact on the world. In 2020 he moved from his home town of Buenos Aires to the coast of Uruguay, where he joined SOS Rescate Fauna Marina, a volunteer-based marine-animal rescue and rehabilitation centre. There, he started working as a volunteer, helping to rehabilitate orphan seal cubs for their return to the wild. Applying the questions and methodologies that inform his practice to his commitment to the rescue centre, Navarro explored the possibility of metamorphosing into a seal to get closer to the animals. The first step he took towards this transformation was to make his appearance resemble that of a seal and to wear a seal suit. The suit is bulky, made of thick, brown foam and latex, and covers the entirety of his body, while his head is covered by a hood; his feet are pushed inside the two large flippers that protrude from the suit; his arms and hands also emerge from thick flippers, and a muzzle with large whiskers covers a substantial part of his face (fig.13).

More than a simple costume, for the artist, this suit is a facilitator of transubstantiation:

> The suit is like a vehicle, in the same way that people put on masks in rituals to access a different way of thinking or seeing the world. Being an artist is a mask in itself that allows a dynamic with society and the universe that is like a kind of bridge. And that mask of being a seal, which is the way you walk, the noise, the fins, the weight, generates a physical condition and at the same time a more spiritual instance of making contact with something greater than the human.[13]

But beyond mimicking the seal's appearance, this prop transforms the artist, conditioning his movements, changing his body temperature, preventing a vertical position and the use of his thumbs, basic anatomic features that played a key role in human evolution. By altering his capacities and skills, the suit makes the artist slightly less human and more seal.

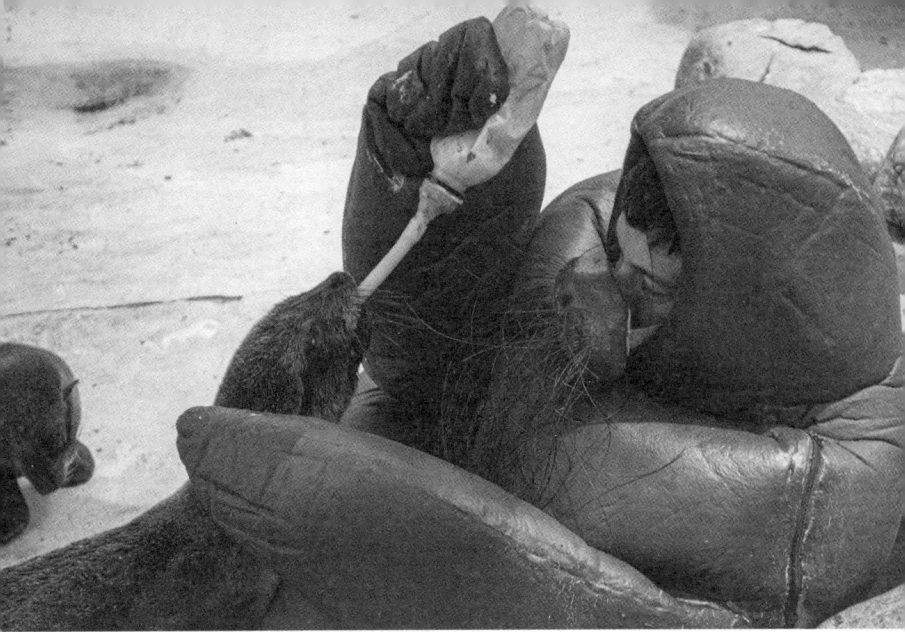

Fig.13 Eduardo Navarro feeding a seal cub at SOS Rescate Fauna Marina in Uruguay as part of his F.O.C.A. project, 2023

COMMUNION

The images that document Navarro wearing the seal costume during the pup feeding sessions are funny and tender, absurd and hopeful. Navarro looks amused and enchanted, but also uncomfortable due to heat, fatigue and the physical constraints of the suit. He is surrounded by seal pups that step on him and drink from the baby bottle he holds. The animals are his only audience: it is for them that he performs these acts of metamorphosis. Such acts are not a ritual, a pantomime or an experience of make-believe. Instead, they carry the hope that, by a process of osmosis, fiction, fun or even through belief, the makeshift seal Navarro incarnates contributes to the improvement of the animals, to their socialisation and nourishment, allowing them to be healthy enough to be released. The whole process could be seen as anthropocentric, as a projection of human needs and affects onto other beings. However, it is actually an experience of decentring the human.

As Navarro reflects:

> For communion to occur I have to come out of my human
> disguise. Breathe, relax, enter another language ... It's
> similar to people with art: you know it's not real but you
> surrender to a belief system, you assume that what the artist
> is channelling is true ... sea lions and seals have a very great
> need to play. And there is a kind of communion between
> two entities that come from different universes. Clearly,
> I don't smell like a seal and I can't exactly imitate the way
> they scream and talk. But they are being empathetic and
> friendly to someone who is in some way surrendering
> to their cosmos.

Navarro's performances are not merely visual. They also
involve a transformation of attitude. During the seal
engagement sessions, he slows down his breathing to enter
a state of relaxation that allows him to endure the discomfort
of the suit, express calmness and induce trust in the animals.
As he explains, 'For communion to occur I have to come out
of my human disguise. Breathe, relax, enter another language.'
Out of this experience, Navarro created F.O.C.A. (Fundación
Oceánica de Contemplación Amorosa, or Foundation for
the Oceanic Contemplation of Affection), supported by the
Santander-based Botín Foundation. The mission of F.O.C.A.
(*foca* in Spanish appropriately means 'seal') is open-ended,
a fact that reveals a deliberate artistic approach to an institution:
the creation of an initiative that, rather than having a concrete
mission and goals, embraces a range of possibilities. Art
becomes a concrete way of focusing on, but also imagining,
different forms of contributing to animal wellbeing: 'I love
not knowing where we are heading with this (me and the
seals). I trust that one day, a spark will bring it all together
in a shareable artistic language of anecdotes – but mainly,
I trust these baby seals will one day go back into the ocean
and have a story worth telling other sea creatures – perhaps
in the most unusual ways too.'

THE ARTIST AS ECOLOGIST

This embrace of the 'not-known', the acceptance of the limits of what is controllable and generated through an artwork and, alongside it, the consciousness that art isn't necessarily 'about' something and that its mission is not pre-defined in its making, is a feature shared by all the artists discussed in this chapter: Jonas; the trio of Barzdžiukaitė, Grainytė and Lapelytė; and Navarro. If the decision to defy an illustrative mission of art and experience was a common feature of the artists whose work was analysed in *Claiming*, and the investment in activating concrete, long-lasting forms of engagement with the land brought together the three artists debated in *Returning*, *Performing* looks at artworks that stand in a delicate and not fully resolved balance between the desire and the reality of triggering environmental change.

This balance isn't merely figurative, it also concerns the fact that all three artists deal with movement and time in a direct manner: using their bodies to perform, sing, dance and even, in the case of Jonas and Navarro, to move like animals of other species. In their individual and unique ways, the three artists take the outstanding legacy of pioneering performers and choreographers such as Anna Halprin, and their engagement with nature and ecology, towards the reality of the present day. They express these matters in an embodied, somatic, physical way. By finding poetic and compelling means to share their grief for the loss of biodiversity in our oceans, as Jonas does in *Moving Off the Land II*; ways to address the paradoxical and contradictory aspects of our lives in the face of climate breakdown, as narrated in the libretto of *Sun & Sea*; and forms of being close to endangered marine animals in order to attempt their recovery, as with Navarro's F.O.C.A. project, the three artists reveal how matters of performing are important in sharing climate-related affects, troubles and preoccupations.

Not being symbolic nor solutionist, their works linger on as invitations to another way of living, to the experimentation with other modes of relating to the self and to others, to desire different things differently. Or simply to be aware of how a body can relate to other bodies. *Reverberating*, the following chapter, will pursue the investigation and discussion of these possibilities within the field of sonic explorations. While temporality remains a fundamental subject, *Reverberating*'s focus on sound, music and ecoacoustics opens up a new prism on the ways in which art contributes to connecting people with other living organisms, capturing and sharing the uniqueness of their environments.

Chapter 4

Reverberating

Reverberating follows *Performing* by pursuing an investigation into how bodies, and the gestures and experiences they produce, act as agents of environmental change within the arts. If the three artists discussed in *Performing* expressed love, wonder and grief towards the natural world, the artists analysed in *Reverberating* conceive sound as a vehicle to reach, interact with and bridge the human and the more-than-human realms, making audiences aware of their existing and potential connections to the planet and all its life forms. Sound has many meanings and manifests itself across an endless array of possibilities. In its extremes, it ranges from noise – a persistent and often disturbing manifestation – to those organised rhythms that are often called music. Sound modulates places, adds character to an environment and sets the tone of a situation. It shapes experiences and encounters. While lacking a physical presence, it can be traced and followed. Sound almost always evades control, as it can be difficult to avoid but also to grasp, which is maybe why it is challenging to define and the terminology employed to do so is often associated with visual patterns and textures, or with onomatopoeic expressions that reproduce rather than describe its effects. This difficulty in describing and transmitting sonic experiences makes them vulnerable to oblivion or misinterpretation. Often, voicing or sounding are considered active, while listening is perceived as a passive mode of engaging with sound.

Tomás Saraceno, Jana Winderen and Carlos Casas, the three artists discussed in this chapter, challenge this logic by activating processes of exchange. They do so not only between themselves and their audiences but also by incorporating the expressive means of nature and creating dynamic relationships that question the directionality of the sources and receptors of sound. As such, they propose that the creation, reverberation and circulation of sound are relational processes that involve all those who participate in them. These processes often make audiences aware of the impact of their presence in the environments and spaces that host them, an awareness that may awaken a sense of responsibility through the recognition of listening as an important practice of sensing the world and attuning oneself to it: a mode of paying attention, responding to and reverberating difference.[1]

TOMÁS SARACENO'S INTERPLANETARY ATTUNEMENTS

For more than two decades, Tomás Saraceno (b.1973) has been making artworks that repair and connect individuals (humans and nonhumans), spaces and relationships. The artist often imagines and proposes forms of cohabitation, of living and existing together, that try to offer a broader perspective on the relationship between the human and more-than-human worlds, inviting people to discover, observe, compose and construct the links between these realities. This interest in using art to activate interspecies and interpersonal relations became evident in Saraceno's practice from 2006 onwards, when his studio undertook research into spiders and their webs, collaborating with biologists, material scientists and other experts from a scientific background, who often joined the team. This research emerged from the artist's interest in the analogy between spiders' webs and the 'cosmic web theory', coined in 1996 by astrophysicist Richard Bond to define the evolution of the structure of the universe through clusters of galaxies connected by webs of filaments that resemble spiders' webs. From his interest in the possible correlation between cosmic and earthly webs, the Spider/ Web Research Group emerged from Saraceno's studio in 2013. It combined art with bioacoustics and biotremology, the study of the vibrations produced by living organisms with a communicative intention.

The initial materialisation of this transdisciplinary approach was the first-ever laser scan of the web of a *Nephila* spider, and the recording of the bouncing signals produced by a *Cyrtophora* (tent-web) spider in a web that has been slightly altered. One year later, in 2014, Saraceno took up a residency at the recently founded Center for Art, Science & Technology (CAST) of the Massachusetts Institute of Technology, a programme dedicated to activating exchange and collaboration among artists, engineers and scientists. This allowed him to pursue his research into spiders and spiders' webs and to further experiment with the use of sound and music to listen to, and connect with, different spiders, in particular those that communicate through drumming (audible vibrations produced with the animals' legs or abdomen).

Embracing the transdisciplinary aims of CAST, Saraceno combined the questions and interests of science with the multiplicity of expressions of art and organised a series of 'concerts' with spiders after the residency. For instance, *Spider Salon* took place in 2014 at the Haus der Kulturen der Welt (HKW) in Berlin, which at the time had positioned itself at the centre of the debate on art, ecology, environmental and social justice, largely thanks to its long-term initiative *The Anthropocene Curriculum* (2013–22). This project revealed how a clear agenda that was both locally rooted and internationally positioned allowed the institution to assert itself in these debates while experimenting with formats: combining discourse, artistic practice and research with multi-layered events where the distinctions between audiences, participants and guests were often blurred.

At HKW, Saraceno brought in an *Eratigena atrica*, a giant house spider, in an open carbon frame which also hosted a sonified web that activated reciprocal processes of sensing, reverberating and tuning-in between various musicians and the spider's vibrations (fig.14). Fitting within this decade-long

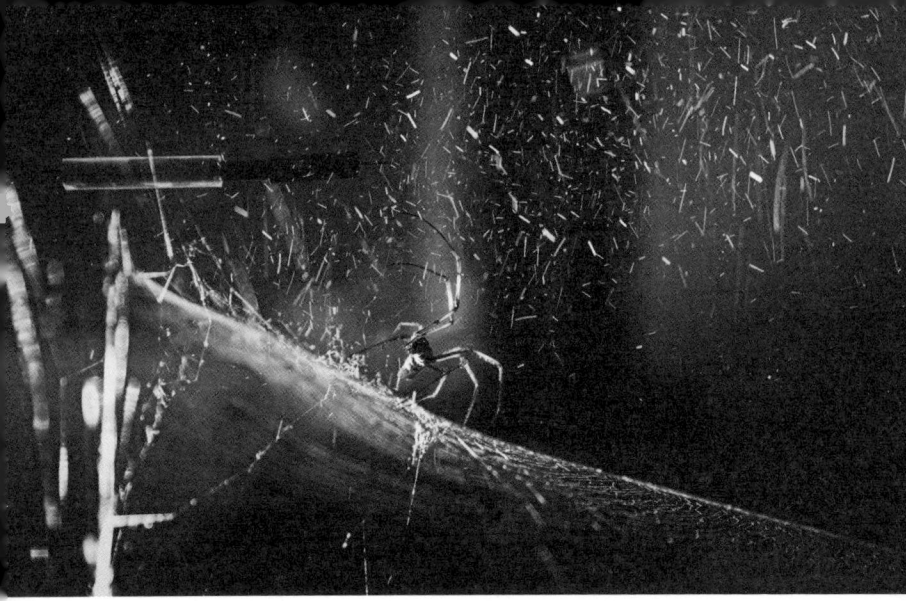

Fig.14 Tomás Saraceno, *Cosmic Dust and the Breathing Ensemble*, 2016.
Installation view during the exhibition *Technosphere × Knowledge*
at Haus der Kulturen der Welt, Berlin, 14-16 April 2016.
Photograph by Studio Tomás Saraceno

initiative aimed at investigating the kind of engagement needed
for a changing planet and at understanding what nature means
in the context of ecological breakdown, the concert was a
meaningful invitation for audiences to engage with a spider
through listening conditions that displaced the human
connection to sound, time and space. Later, during the winter
of 2018–19, Saraceno pursued these investigations in a more
intensive way, when his comprehensive survey exhibition
On Air was held at Paris's Palais de Tokyo.

On Air

Spatially, the display for *On Air* did not follow a linear
trajectory and visitors would often get lost within the large
space of the Palais de Tokyo, one of the largest exhibition
venues in Europe, entangled in its various threads. In tandem
with the exhibition's preparation, and within this area of
Saraceno's work, the term 'entanglement' gained prominence

in contemporary art and culture, in particular following the publication of Karen Barad's book *Meeting the Universe Halfway* in 2007, being used to describe the modes of coexistence of humans and other life forms. In the book, the theoretical physicist and feminist theorist revises and updates quantum physicist Niels Bohr's perspectives on such matters as space, time, matter, agency, subjectivity and causality, proposing that existence is shaped by entanglements. As Barad puts it, 'This book is about entanglements. To be entangled is not simply to be intertwined with another, as in the joining of separate entities, but to lack an independent, self-contained existence. Existence is not an individual affair. Individuals do not pre-exist their interactions; rather, individuals emerge through and as part of their entangled intra-relating.'[2]

One creature of entanglement is the spider, an eight-legged arachnid with a centralised nervous system and an impressive existence of more than 45,000 species spread out across the globe. Spiders' webs, spatial devices that many (but not all) spiders weave, both delicate and complex, are also figures of entanglement. Saraceno dedicated an important part of the exhibition *On Air* to spiders, their constructions and perceptive realms, at times turning the Palais de Tokyo into a space that resembled a natural history museum. Experts from various disciplines – arachnologists, biologists, historians of science, philosophers and composers – were invited to think about, with and near the spiders and their webs. Experimenting with presentation modes that challenged the display codes of contemporary art and kept the exhibition lively and edgy – between a black widow, *Latrodectus mactans*, that was displayed with no protective glass and the intricate, delicate spiders' webs that could disintegrate on human touch – *On Air* focused on the material, cognitive and perceptive realms of these animals. It also considered the ways knowledge about them has been produced and shared, and how it has inspired other areas of research, from astrophysics to material science.

Simultaneously, it investigated the symbolic, affective and emotional dimension of arachnids, taking visitors through various traditions of divination and care for the self that involved spider references and wisdom. These ranged from psychoanalysis to tarot readings using a deck of *Arachnomancy Cards* (2018–ongoing), a set of 33 prophetic cards made by the artist that reveal lucid visions of the present and divinatory messages about the future. This move of the artist's interests towards non-academic epistemological traditions is aligned with the arts and humanities' growth of interest in spirituality, Indigenous world beliefs and other traditions of knowledge-production beyond Western rationalism.

TRANSFORMING TIME

As mentioned, the exhibition's environment was challenging to traverse. Barely lit, it was difficult for visitors to see much when they entered the exhibition at the Palais de Tokyo, with dim light sources directed at the webs as the only orientation reference, guiding people from one spider architecture to another, the illuminated filaments of the webs vibrating in the dark with the movement of air around them. The spiders' webs – an expression of the spider that extends its body in space, organising it without distinguishing the inside from the outside – resembled geodesic domes, fishing nets or cotton candy.

The fact that they looked like something else exposed the associative capacity of human perception, our propensity to avoid the unknown, projecting what is known onto something unclear, as a form of discovering and learning. As also debated in *Performing*, this propensity reveals how anthropomorphism, the humanisation of nature, is a limitation to the possibilities of knowing – humans frequently feel the need to project the behaviours and feelings they know onto other species as a way to comprehend their respective behaviour. But it is also an impulse instilled by a desire to understand and get closer, for it is curiosity in and interest for the other that triggers a speculative projection – the questioning and imagining what another living being may be doing, feeling, thinking or needing.

THE ARTIST AS ECOLOGIST

Traversing these halls of spiders' webs, viewers had a very particular experience of these structures, which can be at once a refuge, a house, a nest, an incubator, an eatable source of protein, an extension of the body, a sensing device, a travelling capsule and a hunting device. Spiders use knitting as a way of making the self, in the sense that the silk used to produce their webs not only comes out of their body but also expands their body in space. Their webs, then, are not merely hunting and housing devices, they are systems of sensing and perceiving the world that decentralise and extend spider cognition.[3] Visiting this part of the exhibition offered an experience of the transformation of time, place and rules. It also required individuals to adopt different bodily behaviour from the typical museum-going stance: to bend downwards and forwards, to curve the neck and legs at unusual angles, barely making any noise, moving slowly and carefully in non-linear patterns.

This navigation through patches of webs led the way to an unusual spider: quite large, red, with long legs, a swollen reddish abdomen, small head and eight eyes. The spider stood so still that it appeared to be dead, yet it was not, a reality as exciting as it was terrifying – large, living spiders are not often found in contemporary art exhibitions. Saraceno had brought to the museum a female *Trichonephila inaurata*, an African red-legged spider, whose scientific name means 'fond of spinning', from the Greek *nein*, to spin, and *philos*, love. The golden thread this *Trichonephila* produces is so strong that sometimes bats and small birds get caught in it.

SPIDERS IN THE MUSEUM

If this was an exceptional encounter, spiders, as well as other small insects (including moths, the terror of conservators), abound in museums, living in pipes, heaters and other infrastructural supports. Generally invisible, they tend to be treated as pests and their presence is seen as a hazard to collections and to an institution's reputation. The fear of insect damage is one of the main reasons why plants were gradually eliminated from exhibitions and museums, where they were widely present until the mid-20th century, as the white cube (a concept coined by critic Brian O'Doherty in 1986 to define the modern exhibition space) became whiter and more aseptic.[4] But at the Palais de Tokyo, Saraceno made the spiders visible, exhibiting them and their webs, also by initiating 'museum spider hunting' sessions that led participants, guided by trained arachnologists, to discover the animals who permanently inhabit the hidden spots of the exhibition space. These sessions were important to reflect on the kind of ecology that a space like the museum holds, and to propose that the coexistence of art and the lives of other species isn't necessarily dangerous or problematic in terms of institutional operations.

The initiative fitted within the wider attempt of the *Arachnophilia* community that Saraceno initiated to desensitise people against a culturally instilled arachnophobia – the fear of spiders – and to raise awareness around the richness and interest of these animals. By allowing this reflection to take place within its premises, the Palais de Tokyo also demonstrated an important capacity for self-reflection and an interest in considering the presence of nonhuman lives within its spaces, something that another Parisian institution, the Pompidou Centre, also explored in 2009 during Pierre Huyghe's retrospective exhibition, which is discussed in the *Exhibiting* chapter, later in this book.

ARACHNOPHILIA

In parallel to these experiences of discovering and engaging with spiders and their processes of worldmaking, Saraceno also used sound to make spiders visible, enhancing their expressive means in ways that were more noticeable to human perception. During the visit to the space, the vibrations of five strings of spider silk, activated by the movement of bodies – those of spiders, visitors, but also of organic and synthetic particles in space – could be heard. These spider filaments resonated with the sound of moving air, highlighting the amount of invisible matter which most people are unaware of, but also its agency, as it responded to and interacted with what surrounded it. An important feature of this installation was how it moved attention from the exhibition's objects to the exhibition's atmosphere, proposing it as an apparatus that exists and has a life of its own, constituted by the various elements, large and small, that traverse it, highlighting the co-dependency of human and nonhuman agencies. Seen this way, the exhibition became not only a model conceived for the presentation of objects and ideas but also an apparatus with a life of its own, impacted by dynamics and flows of particles and beings that exist beyond and above the human perceptive realms.

By providing a non-anthropocentric perspective on a format that has served so strongly to enhance the nature-culture divide, Saraceno contributed to the wider revision of the responsibility of culture in ideologically formatting a world of ontological separations and hierarchies. By determining who was looking and who / what was being looked upon, neatly differentiating subject from object, establishing who had agency and who / what not, and materially separating visitors from collections, exhibitions naturalised differences and distinctions between beings and classes of beings. However, by embracing sound not only to give an environment to an exhibition, but as an actual element that traverses and permeates space and makes visible the invisible, Saraceno reconceptualised the exhibition beyond its human-centric dimension, shedding light on the expressive means of other beings, in their difference and mystery, and their active participation in the complex systems that entangle all people.

This practice touched other realms too: for instance, the *Arachnophilia* symposium held during the show, in which an amplified spiderweb was connected to the sound system of the auditorium in which the scientists and thinkers were gathered, an invitation for the spiders to interrupt the flow of human speech with their drumming. Also, throughout the duration of the exhibition, Saraceno invited three iconic figures from the experimental and avant-garde music scene to play with and for the spiders. Sound artist Alvin Lucier (1931–2021), who dedicated his work to testing the relationship between sound, space and reverberation, performed a *Moon Bounce* concert, in which his heartbeat was transmitted by a sensor routed through the silk strings of a *guqin*, an ancient Chinese stringed instrument, sent to the moon and returned to the Earth two-and-a-half seconds later. This astral reverberation, transmitted from his body across the silk threads of the *guqin* to space and back, was both concrete and unreal, science and magic manifesting themselves through a sound that combined the intimacy of one's own body and an other-worldly realm.

For a concert entitled *The Spider's Canvas*, composer and CAST Director Evan Ziporyn (b.1959) gathered an ensemble to play in and with a spiderweb: 'We play in the canvas of the spider, using sonification of 3D models and 2D images in the harmonic language of Just Intonation. Rather than playing with the spider herself, we are using her webs as the basis of our music, reading her scores, using her geometries as the foundation for our vibrations, she provides us a soundscape through which we can wander', he explained.[5] For a third concert, pioneer electronic music composer Éliane Radigue (b.1932) presented a new version of her *Occam Ocean* series, solo and ensemble pieces for individual instrumentalists that are based on each performer's technique and individual relationship to the instrument they play. Radigue conceived a series of duos, duets and quartets in which instruments and voices emitted low frequencies, played continuously, for long periods, relating to the spiders' sensitive apparatuses. These concerts pursued the exploration of forms of micro- and macro-attunement, rendering the immense and the infinitesimal, the distant and the proximate, the very loud and the inaudible into scales available to human and spider perception.

Jamming with Spiders

With their interest in spider engineering and communication, as well as the correlation between spiders' webs and human conceptions of the cosmos, Saraceno's projects reveal how incredibly complex spiders are, how outlandish is the spider's perspective of the world, and how the structure of the cosmos and other models for grasping the universe are aligned to the structure of spiders' webs. Two of his works, *Galaxies Forming along Filaments, like Droplets along the Strands of a Spider's Web* (2009) and *14 Billions (Working Title)* (2010), testify to this process. Their making was layered and complex, involving among others the NASA International Space Station; the European Science Foundation; researchers from the universities of Darmstadt, Frankfurt and Basel; and Saraceno's studio staff, but their outcome generated straightforward physical and perceptive experiences that acted directly upon the bodies of participating visitors. The works consisted of the 3D scanning and analysis of real webs produced by a black widow spider, in the artist's studio in Berlin, and their transposition to human-scale versions made with nylon ropes. These large, tangled environments made visible that which was previously invisible, either because it was as small and inaccessible as the web of the black widow or as large and abstract as the structure of the universe. These projects led visitors to experience, with their own bodies, the intricacy of spiders' webs.

But visibility isn't always faithful to the complex unfolding of much of earthly and extra-planetary activities. By tuning in to the sensory apparatus shared by many spiders and its reliance on vibration, Saraceno showed how space-time manifests itself through rhythm and movement. Once more, he collaborated with different teams: together, arachnologists, engineers, musicians and different spiders wove a series of museum installations and 'cosmic jam sessions', such as *Cosmic Jive: The Spider Sessions* (2014), *Arachnid Orchestra. Jam Sessions* (2015) or *Jamming with Spiders* (2018). The spiders' strumming and the vibrations of their webs were amplified, recorded, broadcast and mixed with other sounds, galactic resonances captured in space or improvised music. With these interspecies listening sessions and concerts, Saraceno gave voice to all those spiders who – either collectively in the savannah (such as the *Stegodyphus mimosarum*, the African velvet spiders, who live communally, sharing egg and spiderling care, web maintenance, nest defence, prey capture and food consumption) or isolated in the window frames and ceilings of human houses (such as the *Zygiella x-notata*, the silver-sided sector spider, whose females weave a missing sector orb web that contains a single silk line that leads from the orb web to the spider's retreat) – perform 'concerts' that call for a renewed way of seeing and hearing.

JANA WINDEREN'S STRANGENESS

Beyond the more niche audiences of experimental music, the desire also to instil curiosity for and connection with the natural world through a compelling sonic experience for larger audiences was at the root of London's Natural History Museum 2024 Jerwood Foundation commission, extended to Jana Winderen (b.1965), whose immersive sound work pays attention to often hidden and inaccessible expressions of life across the planet. For decades, the artist has been creating rich and layered art-works across multiple formats, from albums that can be listened to remotely, to live performances, concerts and site-specific installations that render the sonic world of living and non-living entities. Through Winderen's work one can hear animals, plants and stones, and often the sounds of animals, such as bats or dolphins, who communicate above 20 kHz, thus beyond the range of human hearing; the passing of elements such as wind or water flowing; biological processes such as photosynthesis and the bubbling of underwater gas; or the sonic landscapes of troubled environments such as salmon aquaculture farms in Norway and the communities of rats living in the port district of Bjørvika, exactly where Futurefarmer's *Flatbread Society* installed its headquarters, as discussed earlier in the chapter *Returning*.

Rather than offering idyllic, pleasant experiences of aural transposition, Winderen's works are often dark, heavily textured and multi-layered, frequently oscillating between periods of intense crackling sounds and others of slow, deep drones. Her compositions and installations take listeners into misty zones of strangeness but also of projection and imagination, expressing a darker side of ecological research. Existing outside language and meaning, beyond representation and images, dealing with sounds that are as concrete as they are undifferentiated and challenging notions of beginning and ending, Winderen's work explores the limits of what may be communicable and expressed when engaging with more-than-human realms. If sound may be a vehicle for the transmission of information and knowledge, Winderen uses it to convey what is unknown, inviting listeners to discover what they have probably never encountered before. She conveys elements that often lie unnoticed by human perception and its emphasis on sight, without reducing them to an anthropocentric experience, without explaining and dissecting them, preventing the sounds she captures and transmits from becoming mere entertainment or educational material, as they preserve their integrity, strangeness and opacity.

The River

This ethos is of course challenged when facing the reality of art's institutional context, with its agendas of inclusivity and its goal of reaching wide audiences, something evident when conceiving an installation for such a highly visited exhibition space as South Kensington's Natural History Museum, which in 2023 drew in more than 5 million visitors.[6] A daily average of nearly 16 thousand visitors forces the museum to cater to needs that bypass content, discourse and experimentation and instead concern entertainment, circulation and accessibility across very diverse age and knowledge groups while managing the safety of visitors and displays alike as well as a good flow and occupation of spaces. As for most audio-visual, time-based installations, whose optimal spectatorship conditions imply silence, calmness and often reduced lighting, Winderen's *The River* (2024) installation inevitably clashed with the institution's audience success, highlighting its limits while proposing that another exhibition experience, one shaped by intimacy and introspection, could be possible and beneficial for such a large institution (fig.15).

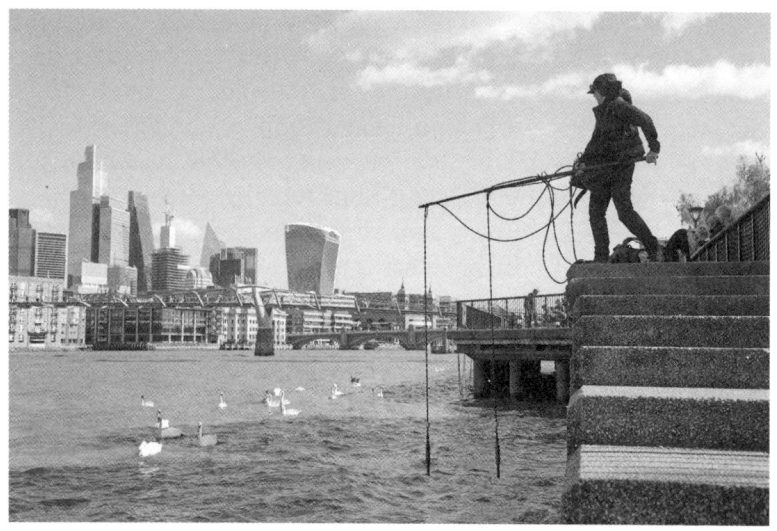

Fig.15   Jana Winderen recording in the River Thames for *The River* commission at the Natural History Museum, London, Winter 2024

The River consists of a 40-minute aural portrait of the River Thames that documents the entangled lives and entities that exist in and across the iconic but highly polluted British river, whose very high levels of viruses and bacteria, excess nutrients, microplastics and other sewage waste threaten its already frail wildlife habitats.[7] Not hiding such contradictions, Winderen recorded the sounds for the installation travelling from source to estuary over five visits and accompanying the seasonal changes that shape its landscapes while incorporating its past and present histories. Culture and ecology, human and more-than-human life, are presented as co-constitutive features whose destinies are profoundly enmeshed. The audio plays on a loop (its beginning and end points are redundant) and its material runs across almost one year of recordings, from the sounds captured in Kemble, at the river's source, in July 2023 to those documented around Queenborough, in the estuary, in April 2024. In Cricklade's shallow waters, Winderen recorded the abstract, round bubbling of methane gas being released from the mud and the sounds of the small oxygen bubbles produced by underwater plants during photosynthesis, which then travel to the water surface. They are interlayered with the crackling of underwater insects, very active during that time of year. This is followed by the artist's recordings around Oxford, where the daily buzz of farms, their animals and machines, and the ducks and other birds that inhabit the region's fluvial nature reserve could have been heard if the artist had not opted for recording exclusively underwater.

This way of making audible what is rarely heard by human ears does not make it any less mysterious and hard to grasp. During two subsequent journeys, Winderen documented the London Thames, traversed by human infrastructure (trains, boats, pumps, sewage facilities), which unsurprisingly created the loudest and most disturbing segment of the whole piece, with metallic and low humming pitches introducing a saturnine mood while signalling how disturbing human presence can be. At the Thames estuary, Winderen encountered seals swimming around such imposing human remains as the World War II Maunsell Forts, indifferent to the fate of human history.[8] The estuary waters can take a few months to finally reach the sea, after eddying back and forth for a while, which creates unique conditions for the distribution and circulation of sound, a suspended temporality that is implied by the piece's slow, arrested pace.

Since it reopened, after a renovation period, in 1999, the Natural History Museum's Jerwood Gallery has been hosting the museum's arts and science exhibition programme. To access Winderen's *The River*, visitors entered a darkened, enclosed space punctuated by benches and beanbags that created the ideal conditions for an extended visit. Surrounding them, a set of 36 speakers, lit by discreet spotlights, formed a multichannel, coordinated Ambisonics system that spatialised a three-dimensional sound field, transposing the different underwater environments recorded by the artist to the space of the Natural History Museum. The Thames rarely felt at once so close and intimate and so strange and disturbing. If the glass vitrines and dioramas that lead the way to the Jerwood Gallery do their best

to explain nature, through *The River* Winderen uses sound
to problematise it, questioning and blurring it in ways which
are intense and mysterious.

CARLOS CASAS'S 'BESTIARI'

A parallel approach was adopted by Carlos Casas (b.1974) in his
multimedia interspecies project *Bestiari*, conceived to represent
Catalonia at the 60th Venice Biennale in 2024 (fig.16).[9] For more
than 20 years, Casas has been making films that engage with
the artistic traditions of documentary cinema and creating
sound pieces and aural environments that trigger new listening
experiences and generate cross-cultural encounters. He has
a longstanding interest in understanding the role of sound in
documenting environments under threat of extinction and
in portraying the interdependencies of humans and nonhumans.
In his work, people and places demonstrate forms of both
mundane and radical existence and cohabitation, as in his
portrait of three people living in solitude in the Tierra del Fuego
in South America (*Solitude at the End of the World*, 2002–5)
or in his documentation of the last residents of Hichigh, a village
in the Pamir mountains on the border between Tajikistan
and Afghanistan (*Avalanche*, 2009–ongoing). Searching for
connections with more-than-human realms, Casas imagined the
death and reincarnation journeys of elephants in the installation
Cemetery, presented at Tate Modern, London, in 2019, and
made a sonic re-enactment of the 1883 eruption of the Krakatoa
volcano (*1883/Krakatoa*, 2021). Across these works, Casas
attempts to find investigative and respectful forms of looking
and listening to bring audiences closer to these subjects while
interrogating the means in which this can be done.

Inspired by Anselm Turmeda's *Disputa de l'ase* [Dispute
of the Donkey], a text which imagines a group of speaking
animals that demand interspecies justice, *Bestiari* is a
hypnagogic environment traversed by sounds and images
of creatures from natural and imagined Catalan landscapes.
The original text, written in 1417 by the Catalan medieval

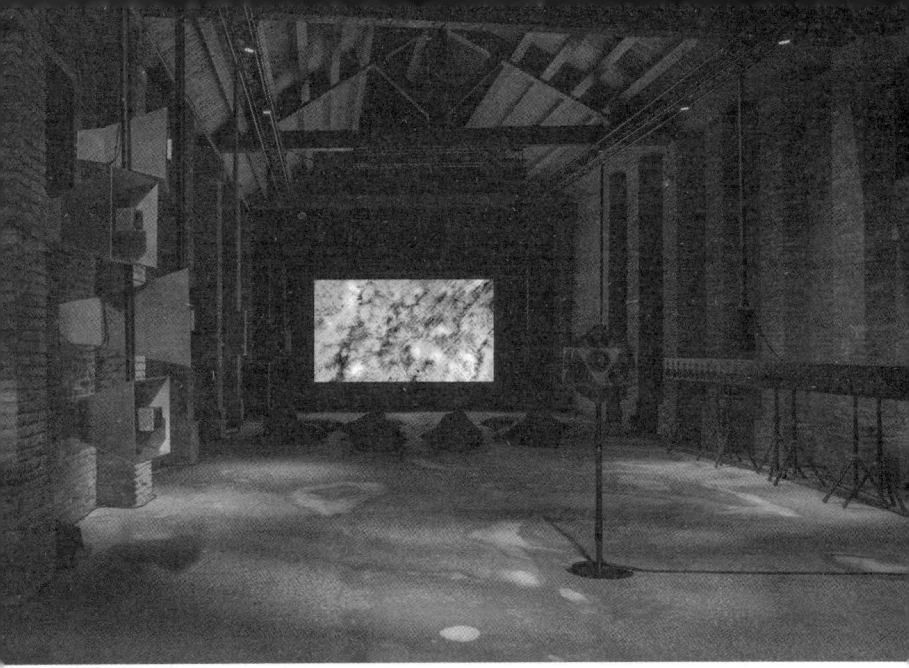

Fig.16   Carlos Casas, *Bestiari*, 2024, installation view of Catalonia Pavilion in Venice during the 60th International Art Exhibition – La Biennale di Venezia, 2024. Photograph by GerdaStudio

author, tells the story of a group of animals who put on trial a man who can understand their languages. Tired of being mistreated, the animals question anthropocentrism, the belief that humans are superior to other animals, quite a progressive initiative for the early 15th century, exemplifying how concerns for animal rights are not a 21st-century invention. As an homage to the animals of the original text, Casas featured sounds and images of bats, bees, dolphins, donkeys, elephants and other creatures recorded in their natural habitats.

This operation of rewriting a medieval narrative may suggest that one upside of the current era of climate unrest is that these are also times of radical questioning. If it was possible for some people to tell stories that paved the way for our state of unecological life, it must also be possible to *un-write* and *re-write* those narratives and expose the myths they propagated. At the top of the long list of necessary revisions lies the entitlement and exceptionalism that certain humans have claimed to have in relation to other humans and to nonhumans. This claim to authority over, and ownership of, others was justified not through material evidence but through aesthetic arguments: proposing that humans are made in the image of the divine allowed those people to feel superior to all other forms of life. Demonstrating that one of the most sophisticated technologies that humans have created to shape the future is storytelling, the centuries-long repetition of this discourse of white exceptionalism led to its activation, a self-fulfilling prophecy. Now, when the weight of plastic on the planet is double that of all animals on earth (humans included) and when there are more creatures going extinct than being discovered for the first time, the narrative of a planet dominated by humans has come to feel real.

Not by chance, *Disputa de l'ase* coincided with the inception of Western modernity, which relied on a worldview that, in order to activate mechanisms of extraction, expansion and consumption, reinforced the division of humans by gender, race and class; of nonhuman beings into species and genres; and of life-manifestations into a separation between what was considered culture and nature. A threshold text, *Disputa de l'ase* challenges but also reinforces the political and philosophical values that consolidate the Modern Project. Lending the text and its author an environmental sensibility while also validating anthropocentrism, this ambiguity reveals an unresolved, conflicted position familiar to many today.

By choosing to follow the 19 arguments of the trial, through which Turmeda reveals his own empathy towards other animals and an awareness of the richness of nonhuman life, Casas enlists Turmeda in current efforts to heal the broken mentality that has led to our troubled planet. This decision is the starting point of *Bestiari*, which bridges the 600 years that separate Turmeda's words and Casas's sounds. The work creates a dreamlike experience in which visitors hear reverberate the cries, clicks, rumbles, murmurs and songs of the creatures that speak along the way.

Bestiari immerses visitors within cycles of images and sounds shot and recorded across several parks of Catalonia. The sound installation offers a dense, multi-sensorial experience featuring visual and audio recordings that extend beyond the range of human sight or hearing. As in Winderen's *The River*, many of the sounds and images recorded have rarely been heard or seen, and their presentation offers an experience that tests the limits of visitors' senses. The Ambisonics 3D sound spatialisation system, as used by Winderen, and the infrasound recordings made by Casas in collaboration with sound artist Chris Watson (b.1953) induce a sense of physical closeness with the animals and natural environments. Unsettling the boundaries of art, cinema and nature recording, the installation attempts to induce corporeal modes of interspecies discovery, revealing how listening can happen through stomach vibrations, or how seeing may be an act of imagining and projecting rather than merely observing.

The various animals are made present through totem-like loudspeakers that establish areas for immersive listening, guiding the circulation of visitors through the space. The film, instead, adopts an investigative animal perspective derived from each animal's spectrum of vision, leading audiences into the worlds created by their different sensorial apparatuses. While attempting to expand and transform our modes of perception, Casas also gets close to the mythological ability of human beings to metamorphose into other creatures. *Bestiari* therefore emerges as an invitation for visitors to embrace the otherness within themselves: to become other, not by mimicking otherness but by internally experiencing what it means to exist as another being through a sensorial transformation.

The three artists discussed in *Reverberating* share an interest in wild and nonhuman life. Through their work, they create ways of paying attention to and recording the sounds of creatures and whole ecosystems that are difficult for most people to access because they are made by animals that are out of reach and that need special equipment to be documented. The spiders that Tomás Saraceno interacts with generally require technical and scientific expertise to locate, identify and record them; the underwater and tidal environments that Jana Winderen records entail long, disciplined listening sessions in harsh situations and places, where the artist faces cold, humidity and discomfort; the sounds of forests and seaside zones that Carlos Casas transposed to his installation *Bestiari* necessitated the collaboration and expertise of a specialist sound artist, as they had to be gathered through listening equipment that can render frequencies beyond the range of human hearing into a perceptible form.

The verb describing how all these sounds were recorded is *captured*, which is intrinsically connected to predation and alienation, to practices of hunting and extracting wildlife from its environment, of transporting it somewhere else. The responsibility and ethos of *capturing* living expressions of animals, plants and nature as a whole are as relevant for the making of artworks of this kind as the conditions in which each artist works and the materials they use. Therefore, the relation to these sonic materials needs to be constantly considered and revised to avoid forms of appropriation and extraction, which only perpetuate the ways in which nature has been instrumentalised and used for human profit throughout the last centuries. Indeed, what makes these projects noteworthy is the sensibility and attention with which they were conceived, developed and presented: the artists' assurance that what is transmitted is not a mere rendering of worlds and lives unknown and distant but a real attempt to unite the sonic realm of nature and humanity, considered as one.

The experiences that these artists produce are engaging, generous and compelling, but they are also demanding, difficult and challenging. They require time, focused attention, silence and contemplation from their audiences. They induce specific modes of listening and sensing and invite the co-creation of new ways of paying attention to the animal and other more-than-human realms. From the exhibition space to the outside world, these artworks propose new ways of hearing and being in tune with nature, of *reverberating* nature, considered not only as a source of entertainment and learning, but as an extension of our own being, which resonates through it and with it. In their own way, these projects explore a mode of declaring our belonging to the connected world, which has been so well conceptualised by Karen Barad: an entangled togetherness in which individuals 'emerge through and as part of their entangled intra-relating'.[10]

Further imagining how to make and present art that is generous and compelling while it also challenges visitors and audiences' expectations and modes of engagement, *Exhibiting*, the following chapter, will introduce and discuss the work of three artists who embraced, and also questioned, the temporal and spatial logic of the museum and exhibition, considered not only as a set of objects and narratives but as an ecology per se.

Chapter 5

Exhibiting

In *Claiming*, *Returning*, *Performing* and *Reverberating* I considered how artists, thanks to their preoccupations and care for the natural world, embraced forms of making art that not only expressed their love and concerns but also proposed and demonstrated that other, more caring and gentle ways of living, both alone and collectively, were possible. In *Exhibiting*, I discuss the well-established format of the exhibition and its imposing logic in the presentation and sharing of art. I debate what happens when consolidated exhibitionary models are rethought in the context of environmental concerns, looking at how certain artists have appropriated and engaged with the exhibition as a whole to make art for and with ecology in mind.

'The dance was frenetic, animated, clattering, twisted, and lasted a long time.' With these words, curator Carolyn Christov-Bakargiev introduced Documenta 13, which she curated in 2012.[1] Taking place in Kassel, Germany, every five years, Documenta has a different history from many global art exhibitions, mostly because it did not emerge from the context of a world's fair and its connection to trade and globalisation, but from Germany's trauma and hope for regeneration that followed the Second World War. Throughout its history, which started with the first edition in 1955, Documenta has attempted to address important questions and lines of enquiry for art and society, and its 13th edition would be no exception. Christov-Bakargiev, alongside a group of international agents and advisors led by curator Chus Martínez, conceived a show that focused on the contingent relationship between people, other beings and things, and how they are activated and traversed by trauma.

For this, she and her team experimented with different formats and modes of presentation which aimed to convey disparate epistemological traditions.

As such, Documenta 13 hosted artworks and discussions that activated, recalled and acknowledged such exchanges. It made space for the dialogue between science and the humanities, gathering disciplines that were not commonly associated with art, publishing the writings and communicating the work of experts from physics, neuroscience, biology or botany alongside art and the humanities. This decision was not only important for the exhibition's outcome, but it also had a major influence on contemporary art's engagement with science and ecology during the following decade, driving the growth of art-related initiatives – from shows to publications and public programmes – that currently intersect art and science and have a specific focus on environmental degradation and reparation. With this, Documenta 13 signalled a turning point in the interests, methodologies and agendas of artists, exhibition makers, authors and institutions, and its spirit is probably felt today more than ever before.

DECENTRALISING KNOWLEDGE

Such assemblages of ideas and lines of enquiry were expressed in the various outputs of the project, comprising publications – 100 notebooks that put side by side the ideas of diverse figures, such as philosopher Judith Butler, anthropologist Michael Taussig, psychoanalyst Melanie Klein, physicist Anton Zeilinger and poet and artist Etel Adnan, to name a few – and the exhibition itself, which took place in different cities (Alexandria / Cairo, Banff, Kabul and Kassel) and across multiple spaces. These included the traditional Documenta exhibition venues, such as the Fridericianum, the documenta-Halle and the Neue Galerie, which were paired with other places with different cultural histories, symbolic weights and traditions of use. The Ottoneum, Kassel's museum of natural history, and the Orangerie, a historical plant conservatory adapted to an astronomy cabinet, demonstrated Documenta's engagement with the natural sciences. This was further reflected in a series of wooden cabins that were spread across the 125 hectares of the city's Karlsaue Park, recalling the vernacular structures for dwelling and living of utopic communes in the early 20th century, while updating the typology of the pavilion and taking visitors for long walks in the public park, beyond the spaces of both old and modern exhibition venues.

With its defence of simplicity, praise of cross-disciplinarity and experimentation with collaborative modes unusual at the time, Documenta 13 introduced new approaches to curatorial and exhibitionary logics. An important aspect of this proposal was the revision and integration of animistic traditions within a curatorial discourse and exhibitionary format. As such, Christov-Bakargiev advanced curator Anselm Franke's investigation of the artificial but naturalised dualistic divisions that shaped Western modernity – explored in his *Animism* exhibition project (2010–12) – and paved the way for her own enquiry and mission to familiarise art audiences with what Franke described as a curatorial exercise of 'revision and decolonisation, not just of the obsolete understanding of animism, but also of the modern imagination'.[2]

Aligned with those concerns, Christov-Bakargiev announced that Documenta 13 would be 'driven by a holistic and non-logocentric vision that is shared with, and recognizes, the knowledges of animate and inanimate makers of the world'.[3] Dogs, insects, bacteria, meteorites and people were considered agents of the show, their contribution seen as complementary and equally important, a consideration made explicit when Christov-Bakargiev stated that Documenta 13 was 'rather the space of relations between people and things, a place of transition and transit between places and *in* places, a political space where the *polis* is not limited by human agency'.[4] Yet, if Franke's *Animism* depended heavily on documentation and theoretical references that might betray the project's call for the revision of the supremacy of Western academic knowledge and followed a classical exhibition and public programme format,

THE ARTIST AS ECOLOGIST

Documenta 13 experimented with sources, places and presentation modes in freer and lighter ways, connecting them more directly with environmental concerns.

REDEFINING EXHIBITIONARY TIME

Christov-Bakargiev's curatorial project supported a redefinition of exhibitionary time that during the years of preparation of Documenta 13 was being experimented with through the integration of dance and performance into the museum (as discussed in the *Performing* chapter). While marking an important step to incorporate practices that had remained peripheral when compared to the institutional attention given to the exhibition of objects (painting, sculpture, photography etc), this move also ran the risk of objectifying performers, who had to work under hard conditions (as with Tino Sehgal's dancers in the dark, who will be discussed later) whilst having short-term contracts. In parallel, visitors would risk being treated as cultural consumers, at once archival repositories and content producers, as they would not only carry within themselves the memories and recollections of the live events they took part in, but also the ways in which these experiences could be turned into online content and shared on social media, supporting an exhibition's communication and outreach strategies. Connected to that, Documenta 13 also reflected on how digital communication technologies and portable phones were altering notions of place, distance and presence, and also of spectatorship, by inducing a sense of simultaneity and a practice of documentation and circulation of content that could disrupt the reliance of the exhibition on the sharing of unique, contingent and rare experiences and encounters, valid both for the presentation of objects and performances.

Tino Sehgal's choreographic work *This Variation* (2012) exemplifies these changes and the decision of the Documenta 13 team to include durational events that happened in parallel and over long periods. In this work, a large group of performers danced uninterruptedly in a dark room at the Huguenot House, in downtown Kassel, throughout the entire duration of the show, being permanently available to visitors, morning to evening, while interacting, in ways that were often gentle and playful but sometimes less so, with visitors who might be amused, confused or slightly uncomfortable. While there seems to have been no curatorial or artistic reflection on the potential exhaustion and mental breakdown of a group of performers who endured dancing in the dark for many hours and days on end, in itself the work addressed and problematically enhanced questions of hyperproductivity, burnout, permanent accessibility and collapse. If these issues were already at the core of the debates around the presentation of performance in the museum, they would also inform many of the concerns intersecting the anticapitalism and environmental protests of the decade to come.

In contrast, *Untilled* by Pierre Huyghe (b.1962) was also a durational and live artwork that investigated the possibilities of exhibitionary time while exploring the conditions that determine an exhibition's life beyond artistic, curatorial and even audience control (fig.17). The title, a pun on *Untitled*, frequently used by contemporary artists to name their works, also expressed a break with the canons of contemporary art and the intention to exit a confined, measurable, aseptic space, be it Brian O'Doherty's white cube or the black box that Sehgal and many others privileged for the presentation of their time-based work. Evolving outdoors, *Untilled* took place (the project avoided such conventional terms as 'exhibited', 'displayed' or 'presented') in a fairly remote area of Karlsaue Park. Unlike other artists who exhibited in the wooden cabins dispersed around the park (including Joan Jonas, whose work is discussed in *Performing*, and Fernando García-Dory, analysed in *Returning*, who transformed an area of the park into an allotment), Huyghe occupied a composting facility, modulating and transforming the area through some subtle and other more imposing interventions that turned it into a strange wasteland, a kind of backstage to the actual exhibition. In it, debris, unwanted and illicit plants (toxic flowers, tobacco, marijuana), living

THE ARTIST AS ECOLOGIST

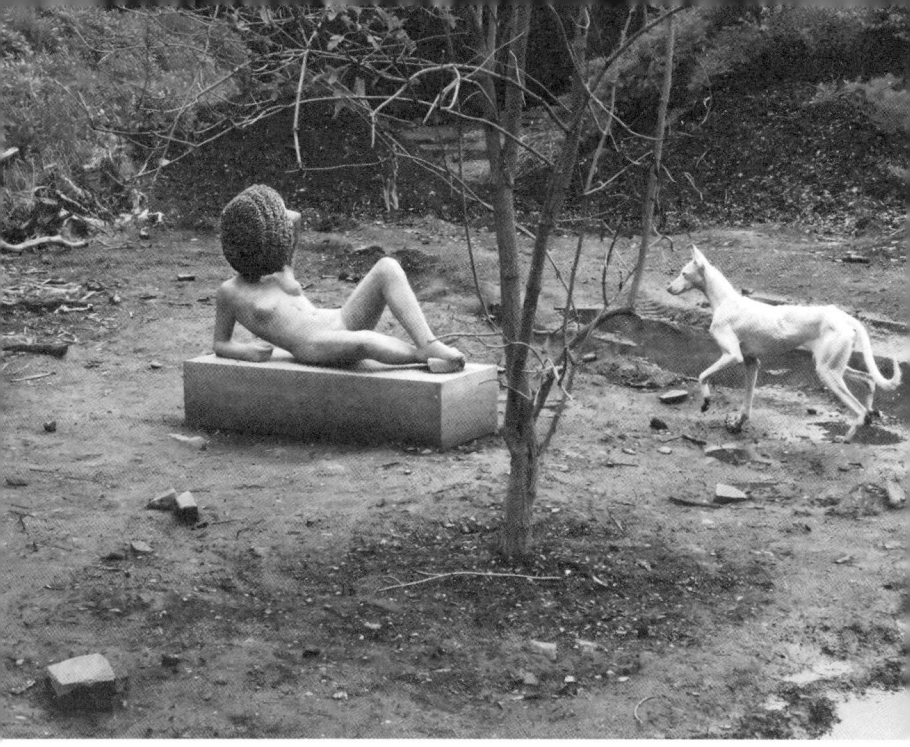

Fig.17   Pierre Huyghe, *Untilled*, 2011–12, living entities and inanimate things, made or not made, including *Untilled (Liegender Frauenakt)*, 2012, concrete cast with beehive structure, wax. Commissioned and presented by Documenta 13 with the support of CIAC, Isabel and Agustin Coppel Collection, Culiacán, Mexico; Fondation Louis Vuitton pour la création, Paris, France; Ishikawa Collection, Okayama, Japan

animals such as a scrawny female dog, her puppy, and the carcasses of the animals that they had eaten coexisted in a system whose opacity and efficiency challenged any human logic system.[5] No billboards signposted the entry to the area and no precise demarcations determined the perimeter of Huyghe's intervention: an experiment without clear beginning or end, suggesting that not even the artist knew how a site in constant mutation would evolve beyond his agency and control.

Visitors were guided to its approximate location by following the indications on the exhibition's map and, once there, they wandered around a space comparable to the environment of Andrei Tarkovsky's film *Stalker* (1979), whose mysterious, posthuman area inhabited by vegetation echoed the obscure, sentient landscape of the Zone.[6] It was difficult to understand what was happening. The expectation of being presented with something that resembled art, behaved like art and was explainable through art's discourse was frustrated, a meaningful challenge to both the exhibition as a format that balances educational, entertainment and pedagogical aims and to the artwork as a product made with an audience in mind. Mediation, which has gradually imposed itself over artistic and curatorial discourses to guarantee that artworks are received and contextualised in an accessible and inclusive way to *all* audiences, was suspended, a decision that created as much surprise and wonder in some visitors as perplexity and frustration in others.

PIERRE HUYGHE'S 'HUMAN'

In this quasi-wasteland, a pile of rubble, various mounds of soil, logs from an old and dried oak tree (one of the *7000 Oaks* Joseph Beuys planted for Documenta 7 in 1982), stacks of building slabs and a load of cobblestones were dispersed amidst growing weeds, an ant colony, a half-dried puddle covered in green algae, and a group of plants cultivated in a more orderly manner. Muddy, indistinct paths led from one cluster of things to the other, and amidst them, intriguing figures with a clearer artistic affiliation emerged. The life-size statue of a reclining nude woman, her head replaced by a beehive, rested on a concrete plinth, a bizarre assemblage of human makings and unmakings – the female nude a trope of classical art history and its instrumentalisation of the feminine body, the beehive a community of insects domesticated for human purposes, concrete a material connected to extractivism and modern infrastructure.

A white dog and her brown pup appeared and disappeared from this environment. Their presence also told a tale of human action: they were *podencos*, also known as Ibizan hounds, ancient Balearic dogs which are bred to hunt but every year

THE ARTIST AS ECOLOGIST

are mistreated, abandoned and killed once the hunting season is over and they are no longer needed. Indeed, the dog had been adopted by Huyghe from a dog rescue organisation in Spain, and the dog's guardian, Marlon Middeke, an environmental engineering student who later became an artist and continued as guardian until the dog's death in 2022, was always nearby, also participating in the environment. A ghostly vision, the dog had a skeletal, emaciated appearance, all her vertebrae visible through her paper-thin white skin. One of her thin front legs was entirely coloured fuchsia, an odd, unnatural colour that enhanced the animal's strangeness and connected her to a large pink bar of concrete that also lay amidst the rubble.

Due to her unsettling but also fascinating looks, the dog, named Human, became one of the most iconic figures of Documenta 13 and of Huyghe's work, also featuring in the artist's 2014 touring retrospective at the Pompidou Centre in Paris, the Museum Ludwig in Cologne and the Los Angeles County Museum of Art. Just as in Kassel, in these exhibitions nothing was expected of the animal other than to be: to walk, sleep, feed and move around at her will, exhibiting her ambivalent nature as an artwork and a ghostly domesticated dog. Even so, Human's presence challenged museum directives and animal rights organisations alike, as a dog in a museum is an uncomfortable presence for those concerned with the museum's security and with animal wellbeing, both groups contesting their respective integrity.

EXHIBITION AS ENCOUNTER

As I have previously written elsewhere while reflecting on Huyghe's presence in Documenta 13, 'no artist could have done this alone. No animal could create such a space. Together, they have woven a new world.'[7] This 'new world' opened a fresh chapter in exhibition history by proposing that the conventional distinctions between subject and object, observer and observed, display and environment, culture and nature, planning and exhibition, could – and should – be shattered. If Franke presented the books, images, films and material testimonies that could break the spell of modernity, Christov-Bakargiev and Huyghe gathered fragments of human infrastructure and a series of unruly creatures to initiate the creation of a hybrid zone in which such distinctions would no longer hold. Through this 'zone of non-knowledge', the artist converted spectators into witnesses of processes that were independent and correlated, regulated and deregulated, observing and participating in a situation they couldn't fully fathom. This event transformed an artwork into a situation and an exhibition into an encounter with the barely known. As the artist put it, 'an encounter should be a deviation ... An exhibition ends, but the work continues and sometimes precedes its appearance. The things exist outside of their exhibition or extend their exhibition. The word exhibition needs to be redefined.'[8]

While refusing its fixed character, the site of *Untilled* is not a creation *ex nihilo*. Instead, it reveals the exponential intensity of what a garden – in its constant tension between human and natural, cultural and auto-generated, wilderness and control, illusion and reality – may host and foster. As such, Huyghe's non-garden resonates with philosopher Michel Foucault's concept of heterotopia and extends it towards a terrain of environmental awareness. Foucault first coined this concept to describe the indescribable. Heterotopias, he argued, are 'disturbing, probably because they secretly undermine language, because they make it impossible to name this and that, because they shatter or tangle common names'.[9] The philosopher would later use the notion of heterotopia to describe the present-day anxious relationship to space-time, in many ways anticipating the disjuncture that was enhanced by the dominance of digital communication devices. He argued that 'the anxiety of our era has to do fundamentally with space', a space that is 'phantasmatic' and is both internal and external to humankind. Heterotopias 'are something like counter-sites, a kind of effectively enacted utopia in which the real sites, all the other real sites that can be found within the culture, are simultaneously represented, contested, and inverted.'[10]

Foucault's heterotopias are places of layered signification devoted to the perpetual accumulation of times. They are environments that juxtapose fragments of different contexts and whose vocation is to induce illusion through the recreation of habitats and situations that are folded into one another, reaching beyond their physical and temporal now: 'The heterotopia is capable of juxtaposing in a single real place several spaces, several sites that are in themselves incompatible'.[11] Foucault's examples of heterotopias range from educational environments (boarding schools), civic engagements (military service, honeymoon trips), institutions of care and confinement (rest homes, psychiatric hospitals, prisons), urban infrastructures (cemeteries, museums, libraries, theatres, cinemas) and the garden, 'the smallest parcel of the world and then it is the totality of the world'.[12] In this non-garden initiated by Huyghe, the layered complexity of time and space come together in ways arbitrary and uneventful, as its only possible monumentality is that of the indifference of nature and its cyclical oscillation between composition and decomposition. It is maybe this non-moralistic, non-propagandistic take on the show's ecological stances, the sharing of a situation, an 'encounter', rather than the production and distribution of information that made *Untilled* so appealing to many, propelling Huyghe to become one of the most established and appreciated artists of his generation.

A Way in Untilled

During Documenta, Huyghe also shot the 14-minute film *A Way in Untilled* (2012), which responds to the situation of the site he initiated at the Karlsaue Park, enhancing and making visible certain viewpoints, zooming in to micro-organisms that coexist with the algae of the pond, filming insects moving above and below the composting soil, recording their movements and sounds, showing Human feeding on an animal carcass, and showing the setting's nocturnal activity. The film is very dark, at parts almost too dark to be seen, and this balance between visibility and opacity generates a tension that displaces the investigation of the function and role of the exhibition towards the sites where the film is presented, generally an art space or cinema. The non-garden's absence of a narrative structure; the induced strangeness and awryness of the place, with its debris and unruly life; and the lack of an aesthetic or conceptual framework to situate the visit within a contemporary art context are also present in the film. The sounds that accompany it, also recorded in situ, oscillate between loud, sharp and violent tones and barely audible rumours. The film portrays the bodies and sounds of the plethora of actors who are for the most part invisible in Huyghe's site, worms and micro-organisms, chemical processes of decomposition. But this documentation is only possible through a close alliance between humans and machines, as it is only thanks to highly sophisticated cameras and microphones that the sounds and images that exist below the human perceptive range are rendered.

During Huyghe's various retrospective exhibitions, the film played while Human, the dog, would traverse the space at will, as if emerging out of the screen, art and reality collapsing into one another and the exhibition becoming an extension of a space of permanent contingency. Nearby, in the same room that hosted the site-specific intervention *Timekeeper* (1999) – a circular form that was created by sandpapering the exhibition walls, an archaeological process to reveal the layers of paint that have accumulated over time – a colony of ants went about their business, circulating across the white space. Their nest had been hidden behind the walls of the museum and they would inhabit this space during the duration of the show. The ants had been lured to the museum so that they could shape the work *Umwelt* [Environment] (2011), an environment created by the co-habitation of 10,000 *Polyrhachis dives* ants with a group of domestic spiders. *Umwelt* defies the aseptic conditions that are expected from such an art space.

In the same area, different spiders walked across the walls. They were part of *C.C. Spider* (2011) (an abbreviation of ceiling corner and not the spider's scientific name) and they were placed there by the artist, the opposite of what Tomás Saraceno did at the Palais de Tokyo when requesting experts to find the spiders that live unseen in the museum, as discussed in *Reverberating*. Under normal circumstances, the museum would employ a disinfestation team to eliminate the animals. Here, they gain a different status, as they are subjected to visitors' gaze, and their presence invites people to pay attention to a kind of life that is generally ignored or seen with suspicion.

Did this experiment manage to bypass the minimal attention granted to such animals and foster a better, friendlier relationship between humans and insects or was it perceived as a conceptual provocation? Maybe the former for some and the latter for many, as the preconceptions concerning most people's relationship to insects and wildlife in general, big or small, will take a long time to be revised and dismantled. They are often surrounded by fear, concern and ignorance – reactions and feelings that are not easily transformed. It will take the joint and continuous action of science, art, education and public-health systems to change the human relationship to the natural world and to those beings whose auras were crystallised by a profoundly entomophobic culture.[13]

None of Huyghe's artworks discussed here are directly advocating for animal or environmental justice. They are not even offering active information channels about the lives they involve and the ecosystems they are interacting with or generating. These works are opaque, strange, difficult to grasp and often so subtle that their mere existence challenges the definition of an exhibition. Yet, in their call for a different sensibility, for a different way of seeing and sensing the environments that surround us, they appeal for the transformation, if not expansion, of our human sensory and perceptive realm, while asking for attention and delicacy towards the places they stand upon and propitiate. The site of the exhibition becomes at once more vibrant, more surprising and more fragile, for it can be easily ignored, stepped upon or destroyed. And at the same time, it is the whole outside world – the space that exists beyond the threshold of the museum and exhibition site – that opens itself in its potential to be seen and considered, even in its most underwhelming, minimal presences. Such humane transformation of the aseptic environment where an exhibition can happen (rather than merely be presented), alongside the propagation of encounters whose stories shift narrative, emotional and cognitive realms (as in *Untilled* and *A Way in Untilled*), are crucial in changing mindsets and helping to dismantle the dualisms of Western modernity.

THE SEVENTH CONTINENT

Attempting actively to explore the ways in which art can participate in the debates surrounding the climate crisis in a straightforward way, the 16th Istanbul Biennial (2019), curated by critic Nicolas Bourriaud, was entitled *The Seventh Continent*. Its title was borrowed from the Great Pacific Garbage Patch, an island of plastic waste located in the waters of the Northern Pacific Ocean, formed by oceanic currents that bring together a vast assemblage of debris. More than three million square kilometres (more than three times the size of the UK) concentrate almost eight million tons of floating plastic, a waste island that ironically houses a large amount of species, mostly marine invertebrates.[14] A continent of debris which was formed through plastic's everlasting materiality and which, like Huyghe's project, no human, animal or geological force could have created alone but which is shaped by the triangulation of unpredictable and uncontrollable agencies. Finding a consensual name for monstrous assemblages like these has been difficult, as there is always something hyperbolic or inaccurate in the many descriptors proposed.

Despite its generalising potential – generalising because not all *Anthropos* are alike and equally responsible for climate breakdown – the Anthropocene became a widespread concept to describe this situation in academic, artistic and popular media contexts. Coined as a term by limnologist Eugene Stoermer and atmospheric chemist Paul Crutzen in 2000, at the dawn of the millennium, the Anthropocene attested to their evidence that human activity across the planet has been so prevalent that it inaugurated a new geological era. The term quickly surpassed the scientific milieu, becoming a widely used cultural concept that Bourriaud borrowed as a guiding reference for the theoretical framework of the 2019 Istanbul Biennial, where the Anthropocene was treated as a theme rather than a new way of making exhibitions. Bourriaud created a conventional exhibition that was well curated but more illustrative than persuasive. Despite this, the show had core sections that tackled the issues raised by the concept of the Anthropocene, problematising, investigating and debating them in a transdisciplinary way which demonstrated the advantages of bringing together the epistemologies of the sciences and the humanities. One of the projects that better contributed to such an approach was that of Feral Atlas.

FERAL ATLAS

Founded in the 2010s, Feral Atlas describes itself as a 'collaborative project involving scientists, scholars, artists, poets and vernacular and Indigenous observers of the Anthropocene'.[15] Unlike most practices discussed here, Feral Atlas is a collective made up of individuals from many different backgrounds, and the artists who are part of it are only a small fraction of the whole. Yet they are often invited to present their work in the context of art, taking part in discussion panels and symposia, publications and exhibitions where their research is considered for its artistic value and presented in formats that are aligned with the aesthetics of contemporary art. At the 16th Istanbul Biennial, Feral Atlas exhibited a series of case-studies of 'feral manifestations'. By 'feral', the collective means the processes that emerge through human-led activities (for instance, the displacement of materials and organisms, terraforming programmes, logistic operations, the release of organisms and toxic components onto the land, the simplification of biodiversity in industrial agriculture, and their various interactions) but which are not within the control of humans

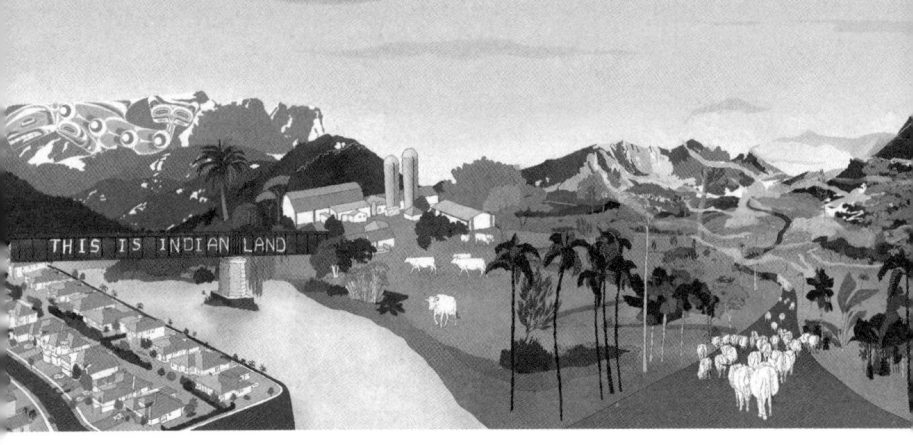

and which affect the organisation of natural systems in dispersed ways. The collective documents these 'feral manifestations' through various processes and methodologies and combines the knowledge of scientists, ecologists, artists and anthropologists (Anna L. Tsing, one of Feral Atlas's curator-editors, is a key voice in contemporary anthropology and beloved as an author in the contemporary art environment, following the success of her 2015 book *The Mushroom at the End of the World*, which discusses the possibility of life in the ruins of capitalism).

Presented at the MSFAU Istanbul Museum of Painting and Sculpture (created in 1937 to conserve and display modern Turkish art), Feral Atlas's exhibition was one of the most rewarding and coherent responses to the curatorial concept of the show. Their section was dense with information, research materials and data, a strategy that can overwhelm and frustrate visitors in demanding a high attention span and forcing them to face their own limits and responsibilities in relation to the reality of ecological collapse. In terms of display, nothing particularly original emerged from Feral Atlas's exhibition choices. The *Anthropocene Curriculum* research project conducted by Berlin's Haus der Kulturen der Welt mentioned in *Reverberating*, for instance, also largely relied on a similar format for its presentation. Yet, the introduction, popularisation and diffusion of the concept of ferality,

THE ARTIST AS ECOLOGIST

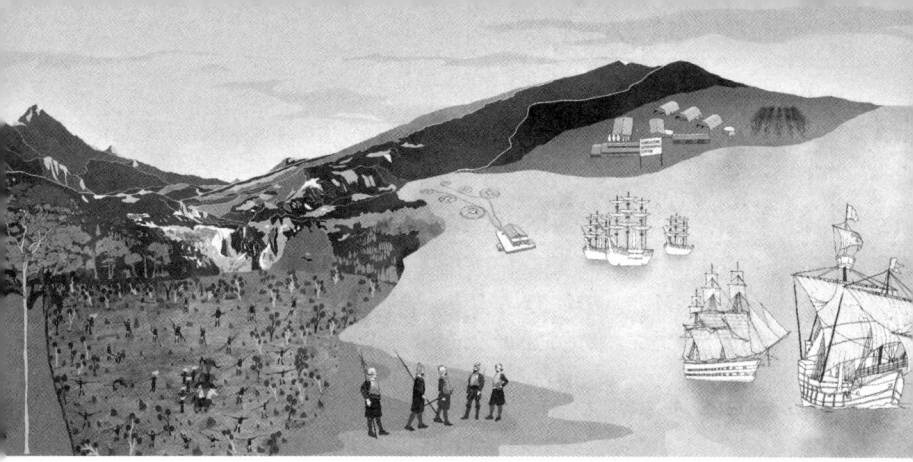

as proposed by Tsing and her Feral Atlas partners, as well
as the interest in engaging with such an historically charged
format as the exhibition through figurations (imagined and
real representations comprising drawings, maps, diagrams)
and compelling modes of storytelling, signalled an important
upgrade in the intersection of academic, curatorial and artistic
realms. Thanks to this presentation, the Istanbul Biennale
participated in the most important advances concerning
ecology and the arts of the time.

BEINGS IN BEINGS

In Feral Atlas's exhibition for the 2019 Istanbul Biennial,
the large maps drawn by Feifei Zhou depicted the impact
of imperial and industrial infrastructures on individuals
(human and nonhuman) and territories by highlighting,
through drawings and watercolours, concrete lines and zones
of entanglement, erosion and production of 'feral phenomena'
(fig.18). Feral entities vary in time and context. The strains
of *Aedes aegypti* mosquitoes that emerged from slave ships
and carry present-day diseases such as dengue or zika; the
introduction of American bullfrogs into Asian and Latin
American environments and their endangering of native fauna;
the contamination of the Jakarta Bay in Indonesia by domestic,

Fig.18   Feifei Zhou with Nancy McDinny and Andy Everson,
Invasion (detail), 2020

industrial and agricultural discharges; and the emergence of *Perna viridis*, the Asian green mussels which absorb and, when ingested, redistribute toxins and heavy metals: these are all feral processes that the collective presented and made visible through maps, films, texts and slideshows.

Rather than merely illustrating these situations and pointing the finger at their instigators, these renderings attest to the importance of the joint work of contributors from various disciplinary backgrounds and historically situate these different narratives, building chronologies and maps that are as linear as they are fragmented, or 'patched', to use their own terminology. Zhou's maps – a crucial part of the project's imagery – depict territories at a stage when the troubled relationships between bodies and history unfold. Drafting cartographies of environmental and social disarray, her maps and drawings reveal how humans are in no way separated from the ecologies they disturb. Instead of inculpating viewers, highlighting their responsibility in the messy situations they portray, they invite a different conception of what it is to live, making people aware of how they are part of an unruly family of outlandish, cosmic, dangerous and interdependent creatures onboard planet Earth: beings in beings.

ANICKA YI'S SHARED WORLD

Those creatures that affect and belong to the world can also be cyborgs, machines that by moving and reacting to their surroundings participate in the living realm. 'What would it feel like to share the world with machines that could live in the wild and evolve on their own?' was the question that, in a slightly different context, Anicka Yi (b.1971) asked, as a starting point for her installation *In Love with the World* for the Winter 2021 Hyundai Commission for the Turbine Hall at Tate Modern in London. The artist created a series of translucent balloons equipped with drone engines and commanded by an interactive mobility AI. The balloons were called 'aerobes', a term borrowed from biology, where it defines

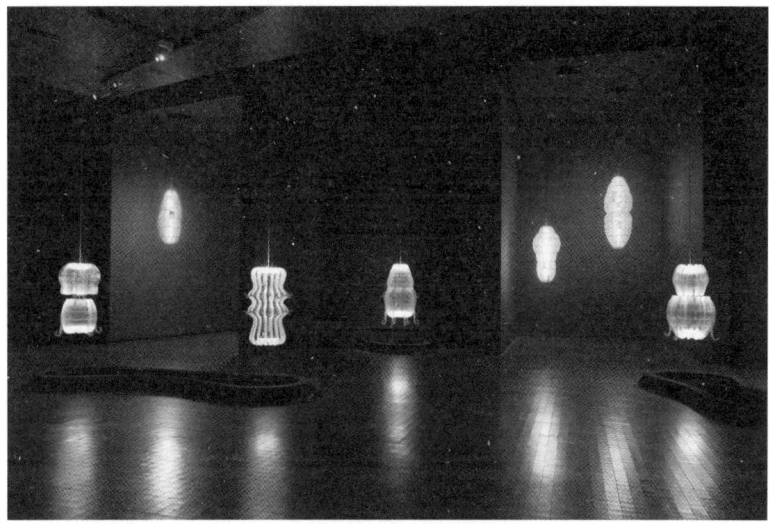

Fig.19   Anicka Yi, *There Exists Another Evolution, But In This One*,
Leeum Museum of Art, Seoul, 2024. Photograph by Andrea Rossetti

airborne micro-organisms, such as bacteria or yeast, that
depend on oxygen for growth and metabolism. Yi's aerobes,
instead, were the size of a large paper lantern and had
a cephalopod and mushroom-like appearance. The artist has
made similar forms in other artworks. Such was the case of the
series of works presented in *Biologizing the Machine (Tentacular
Trouble)* – yellow, cocoon-like lanterns made of kelp, acrylic,
animatronic moths, concrete and water that were hanging
in the Arsenale during the 58th Venice Biennale (2019). During
There Exists Another Evolution, But In This One (fig.19), her
solo exhibition at Seoul's Leeum Museum (2024), Yi displayed
a series of animatronic sculptures entitled *Radiolaria* (a name
that refers to single-celled zooplankton organisms that emerged
during the Cambrian period, about 500 million years ago),
which seem to have a life of their own, moving, vibrating and
pulsating in ways that defy the machine-organic life thresholds.

At Tate Modern, the aerobes were gently propelled into the
air by a series of small fans making low humming noises. Slowly
swarming across the 35 m (115 ft) high Turbine Hall, the aerobes

enchanted audiences with their outlandish looks and delicate choreographies. Even if human-run, their movement defied reason and an anthropocentric sense of agency, movement and dance. Looking like and acting like animals as much as machines, they dissolved ontological divisions that separate what is living from what is not. As such, they transformed the Turbine Hall into the set of a sci-fi narrative: a hangar where flying cephalopod robots posed many questions to its visitors: What were they doing there? How did they move? What worlds could they form, and stories could they tell?

Commenting on the project, the artist expressed how 'I wanted to think about the industrial history of the Turbine Hall and how it was used to convert energy for machines'.[16] Tate Modern's home is the converted former Bankside Power Station (the last electricity-producing operation of central London), and its Turbine Hall is framed by the traces of industrialisation preserved by architects Herzog & de Meuron during their renovation of the building, which opened as Tate Modern in 2000. But if indeed the aerobes were to relate to the industrial past of the power plant, these drones would only reinforce human reliance on and fascination with machines and energy. They would update the mastodontic, polluting beast that was the power station and its fuelling of urban productivity, transferring it to a distributed, minimal and seemingly clean swarm of robotic creatures that turn energy into entertainment and wonder.

If the original building survived and its industrial past has been kept alive through the spatial denominations that the Tate preserved – the Turbine Hall, Switch House and Tanks – Yi's aerobes also engage with longevity through their material constituents. With plastic, humans reinvented immortality by creating a material whose lifespan largely surpasses their own. Like the power plant's architecture, these creatures will continue their material life beyond their demise.[17] In addition, and recalling artist Hito Steyerl's investigation of the museum as the new factory – as in her 2009 text 'Is a Museum a Factory?', in which she observed the number

THE ARTIST AS ECOLOGIST

of contemporary art museums that now occupy disused industrial buildings as forms of cultural and artistic labour replace the industrial workforce – the aerobes would not be collaborating with and performing for the audiences: they would be further persuading the audience to produce and consume.[18] The political life of these quasi-creatures would be aligned with the building's history and its economic mission to fuel and increase human productivity.

Yet, the aerobes, beyond their taxonomic allusion to biology, beyond their situatedness in a revamped industrial site, beyond the events that Yi created to support them (for example, the 'scentscapes' diffused by the artist evoking the foul odours of the Industrial Age and of medieval medicinal spices used against the Black Death pandemic), triggered curiosity, joy and a sense of other-worldliness that bypassed any institutional mediation or conceptual discourse. They challenged comprehension and offered fantasy, their numbers being too limited to create an immersive experience but enough to transform the Turbine Hall into a space of fiction where other stories about machine and human interaction might be told. These stories can be sombre, recalling how animals have been instrumentalised and considered machines by the Cartesian mind. They also call to mind the many machines and technologies that were inspired by animals, from engines that run on 'horsepower' to drones that resemble and sound like flying insects, and wind turbines whose aerodynamic shape is inspired by the fins of humpback whales, to name but a few.

Taking this confluence, one could say that every machine was once an animal: the story it tells is inevitably about serving human purposes and its shape bears traces of zoomorphism.[19] The stories that the aerobes tell may also be strange and intriguing, immersing visitors in other planetary realms and proposing new communities, in which humans, animals and machines coexist beyond taxonomic divisions. Positive or negative, these stories are never fully told, they are not necessarily 'about' something and they are not delivered through facile, linear narratives. This resistance to simplification concerning art in its intersection of ecology is a matter of particular importance in a moment, such as the current one, in which there is a profusion of large-scale exhibitions that propose 'immersive', 'multisensory', and 'interactive' experiences, while often treating visitors as consumers of a pre-packaged spectacle.

OTHER SPACES

The exhibition is a highly charged format. By conceiving of the exhibition as an environment (rather than a mere space, or a sequence of spaces, to occupy) and allowing it to be dynamic, in flux and responsive, Yi rethought and decoded its logic, opening it up to other possibilities and to the unfolding of unexpected situations. This is a meaningful operation in a moment in which such 'immersive' exhibitions largely rely on VR and 3D headset simulations of artworks, places and situations, and whose reliance on technology could align with Tate's *In Love with the World*. Yet there is a striking difference. Most offer interactive audio-visual experiences that balance the celebration of the natural world with a few glimpses of eco-consciousness and with televised entertainment. Such is the case with *Visions of Nature: A mixed reality experience*, a VR journey presented at London's Natural History Museum since 2024, or the Smithsonian Institution in Washington DC's touring exhibition *No Spectators: The Art of Burning Man* (2018–20), a revisitation of the North American Burning Man desert festival.

The stories that Yi's aerobes inspire, as well as those that emerge from the encounter with Feral Atlas's accounts and Pierre Huyghe's puzzling spaces, contrast with these graphic technological experiences of re-creation and entertainment, digested for mass audiences. They do not propose characters or represent places and situations. They do not talk about the weather, or illustrate stories of climate catastrophe or the natural sublime. In their subtlety, thanks to the constant movement and reconfiguration of the figures, relationships and situations that they bring together, they call for specific forms of apperception, asking visitors to use attention as an instrument to tune in to what is happening around them, to what unfolds, moves or reveals itself quietly, discreetly. They defy the logics of spectacle by proposing that nature tells no stories, that it is not there to entertain, educate or be extracted from. The landscapes they compose, be they the intricate maps drafted by Feral Atlas's Feifei Zhou or the reconfigurations of wastelands set in place by Pierre Huyghe or Anicka Yi's aerobes adrift across Tate Modern's Turbine Hall, can initiate transformative experiences that act upon the space, the audiences and also upon an exhibition's inner grammar and structure.

These transformations are not attempting to explain and illustrate ecology, science or climate breakdown. Instead, in their depth and strangeness they are making their own versions of worlds, as meaningful, valid and important as those provided by the epistemological traditions of the sciences and humanities. As such, they carry the potential to profoundly touch and transform those who experience them. To instil dances – a powerful term to address a state of mental and emotional rupture and transformation – that, echoing Christov-Bakargiev's words, are frenetic, animated, clattering, twisted and enduring.

Art for the Present-Future

In 2012 curator Carolyn Christov-Bakargiev announced that
the Documenta 13 project she had conceived had two processes
as a reference: collapse and recovery. Despite the implicit
correlation between the two, suggesting that birth follows
decay, she offered a more nuanced proposal, acknowledging
how 'collapse and recovery no longer seem two subsequent
moments in time, but often appear simultaneously'.[1] This
possibility has also been explored by Feral Atlas's cofounder,
anthropologist Anna L. Tsing, in her conceptualisation
of the 'patchy Anthropocene', acknowledging that in the
current geological era, humans and nonhumans share uneven,
misaligned landscapes and rhythms.[2] Christov-Bakargiev
envisaged the co-dependency between the two movements
of collapse and recovery, assuming that, although disturbed,
they continued to complement one another. Even when one
would not follow the other, or something would not necessarily
emerge from the ruins of something else, the possibility
of the coexistence of collapse and recovery still suggested that
regeneration would happen – an extension of the empirical
tradition that sees life emerging from decay, composition
and decomposition being conceived as dependent entities.
This meant that the cause-effect cycle continued to operate,
albeit in a broken and uneven way.

   Only a decade later, in the light of the current scale
of planetary breakdown, does this dynamic of collapse and
regeneration, in its cyclicality or concurrent manifestation,
appear naive and overly optimistic. It no longer holds. In 2022,
ten years after Christov-Bakargiev's proposal, historian Adam

Tooze popularised the notion of *polycrisis* to argue that a world so profoundly interconnected and vulnerable as ours is also much more prone to hosting catastrophes that quickly become interconnected and that have few healing possibilities, given how fragile natural and social systems currently are.[3] This is a world that is struggling to hold and absorb trouble and to recover from the trauma resulting from it. Inevitably, the cycle that brought together collapse and recovery is interrupted. This rupture also creates a crisis of imagination, as it is hard to live with this awareness; to move forward and discover where and how to find hope and energy; to continue longing for change when change itself has become synonymous with decay and not regeneration; to move ahead when loss seems to be everywhere, particularly in the future. It is thus not surprising that grief is so present in people's minds and hearts. Some, like writer Vanessa Machado de Oliveira, find hope in imagining how to care for a dying modernity and its obsolete narrative of linear progress and growth, acknowledging that what follows is not regeneration, transformation into something better, but the unknown.[4] The sole hope seems to rely on the possibility that better and wiser systems will arise from this death, but even that isn't certain.

THE UNKNOWN

It is hard to envisage a dying modernity without knowing what comes next. It requires an unknown language and the courage to face the gradual subsidence of safe, comfortable structures that were long taken for granted. 'Learning to offer palliative care to modernity dying within and around us is not something that modernity itself can teach us to do', Machado de Oliveira argues.[5] This proposal offers a silver lining to the realisation that recovery no longer follows collapse, as it presents rupture as the way towards a different mindset, one that does not inherit the vices and conceptions of the past but that instead leads the way towards an unknown future order. Accompanying us through grief and along the palliative journey, art appears

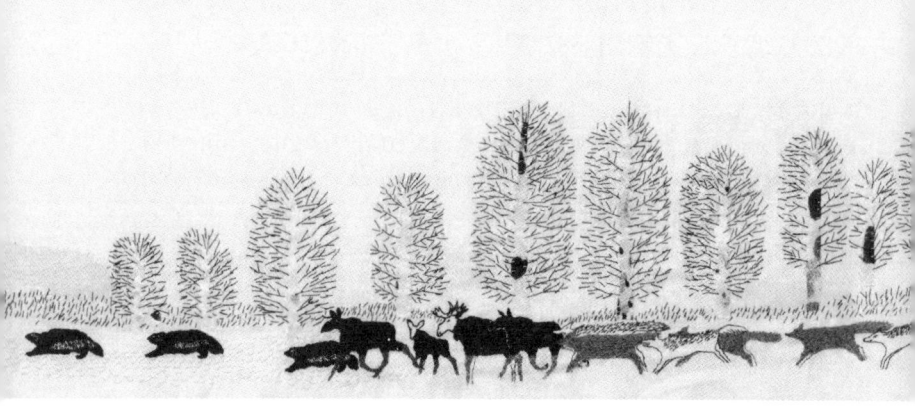

as a crucial partner in pain and imagination. Each in their own way, through practices and forms that are distinct yet complementary, the artists discussed in this book face a damaged world with their art and have initiated individual and collective experiences of transformation that may help to trace a path that is in tune with nature, its losses and outcomes.

I opted not to touch upon matters of loss and grief in the book's introduction because I did not want to impose such a strong reading on forms of art that are as active, imaginative, lucid and full of optimism as the ones that have been described here. These final notes may add a darker tone to the publication as a whole, but they also ground it in the acknowledgement of the troubled times we experience. A book about art and ecology would be unrealistic if it only provided positive examples of care and transformation. Conversely, a discussion that only touched upon concerns about the troubled planet might have triggered negative responses, a sense of guilt and frustration that generates paralysis and despair rather than providing possible positive outcomes, even if unknown, as Machado de Oliveira argues. Throughout these five chapters, I have proposed that the ways in which art may radically

THE ARTIST AS ECOLOGIST

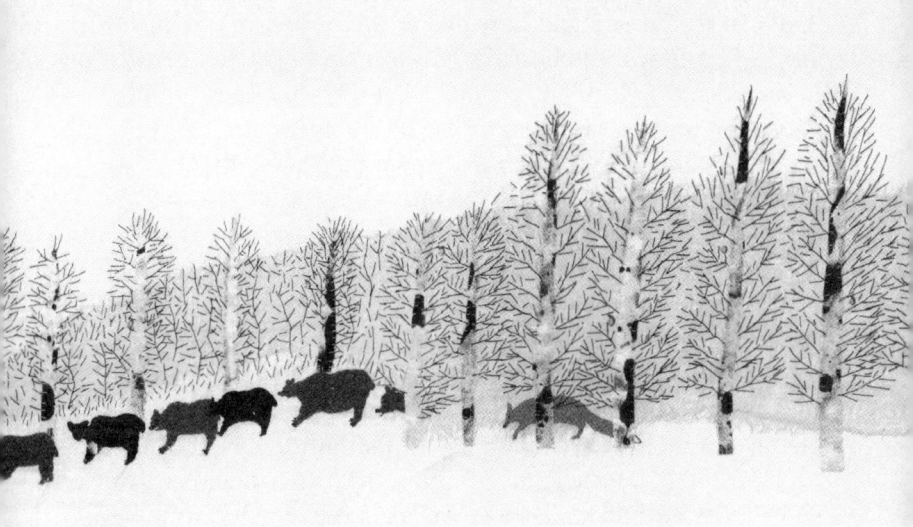

question the given world, by leading what is known into the unknown, di-systematising methodologies, inventing procedures and challenging given representations and placements, are fundamental in this exercise of courage, of openness to what may follow the known world. In their different and unique ways, the artists that have been discussed all seem willing to help us do so.

The opening chapter, *Claiming*, discussed the work of the members of the collective COUSIN and the ways in which they often refuse to present digested, facile and literal representations of individual and collective Indigenous experiences. Working primarily with moving images, they are aware of the delicate balance between privacy and sharing, between revealing (and creating) experiences of joy and celebration of Indigenous life and going beyond what others may want to share and disclose. The negotiation between what can be, should be and *is* seen and what finds no place to be explained and illustrated is a constant feature of the work COUSIN's members make and support. When interviewed, COUSIN cofounder Sky Hopinka explained how 'I don't film anything that isn't meant to be filmed ...

Fig.20   Fragment of Britta Marakatt-Labba's embroidery
Historjá [History], 2003–7

[I'm] just thinking about how people are presenting themselves, and how they want to be seen, and what am I getting permission to record and to film and to look at. It feels like there's a play between the two.'[6] Indeed, COUSIN's politics of opacity, carefully balancing consent and spontaneity, experience and exhibition, do an important job of revising ethnographic cinema and its complex implications in colonialism, imperialism and extractivism, in and beyond academia and the arts. They reveal how the acceptance of the unknown is key for relationships to be established across people coming from diverse backgrounds and experiences, and how this unknown element may frame both a relationship with the past and present but also be a tool to accepting what the future may bring.

Invested in another sort of unknown, that which permeates spirituality and mysticism, as well as a relationship to the land, is Tabita Rezaire, whose project Amakaba is introduced in the chapter *Returning*. Investigating how to find one's identity and sense of belonging through practices that combine food production and healing traditions, Amakaba was initiated by the artist during the COVID-19 pandemic. Amakaba unites two activities that are seldom brought together: daydreaming and work, revealing how they actually complement one another. When creating Amakaba, Rezaire moved from Paris to her father's home country of French Guiana, which allowed her to explore concrete, long-term forms of decolonial healing in a project that hosts an 11-hectare cacao farm managed with an agroecological approach, doula-training activities and a moon centre dedicated to both astrological and astronomic knowledge.

At the same time as Rezaire's Amakaba was starting out, artist Eduardo Navarro also moved from his home town of Buenos Aires to the coast of Uruguay, where he benefitted from the pandemic hiatus to collaborate with a local seal-rescue centre. If Rezaire found in the physical and metaphysical relationship to the land a form of practising decolonial healing, Navarro dedicated himself to these animals, in particular to the seal pups who were brought to the centre and needed feeding and attention. In many of his previous works, the artist had created suits and costumes that allowed him to get closer to other life forms. During the 2015 New Museum Triennale (held in New York), he was inspired by the writings of autism and animal activist Temple Grandin – who argues that animals think through images – and sought to understand a turtle's relationship to time and space (*Timeless Alex*). For this piece, he had created a turtle sculpture that he wore during a two-hour performance in which he attempted to move slower than language so as to reach a nonhuman mindset. In Uruguay, the artist created a seal suit that constrained his mobility and made him seal-like, imagining the amusement and empathy of the seals. 'The suit is a vehicle, not a costume', he argued,[7] a conception that placed his work in concordance with symbiotic, artistic and scientific realms, recalling both the wildlife teams that wear animal suits in conservation efforts and performance artists' engagement with nonhuman representations, from Peter Fischli and David Weiss to Joan Jonas, whose work is also discussed in the *Performing* chapter.

Reverberating further extends the debate about the ways in which art approaches and invites us to get closer to nature. Discussing three artists who work with sound and create audio environments from spaces and creatures that are generally disregarded or out of reach, the chapter analysed the work of Jana Winderen, in particular *The River*, a sound installation commissioned by London's Natural History Museum. *The River* does not attempt to provide a contemplative representation of the River Thames or a scientific illustration of its ecology, akin to the specimens presented at this historical venue. Instead, it moves spectators-turned-listeners in and out of its waters through an assemblage of sounds mysterious and uncanny, which range from the popping of gas bubbles released by aquatic plants to the drones of speed boats traversing the river's busiest areas. Without providing a narrative, and thus challenging the assumption that nature tells stories and nonhuman life can be rendered through art, Winderen's installation operates within a regime of opacity parallel to that of COUSIN. While the experience of entering a dark, calm, cocooned space is comforting and reassuring – providing solace from the masses that every day visit this very popular museum – it also resists acting as an immersive experience of passive spectatorship. The strangeness of the sounds presented, their circulation across the space through a dynamic system of sound spatialisation called Ambisonics, the absence of the human voice and of any explanations, all call for an engagement that, being dynamic, provides individual, singular encounters which modulate the conventional uses of our senses, inviting us to perceive and, why not, to exist in other ways.

Aligned with this resistance to explaining and digesting nature through art is Pierre Huyghe's environment *Untilled*, created for Documenta 13 in 2012. Alongside several others, this project demonstrated the pioneering ecological stances of Christov-Bakargiev's curatorial project, whose legacy is still present today, and it was probably the exhibition that furthered her agenda the most. Huyghe's work, in particular the contribution of Human, its iconic white dog with a fuchsia leg, became a reference point for those interested in understanding the relationship between living organisms and fabricated materials, and the ways they may coexist, affect and shape one another. This cinematic non-space, which evoked Tarkovsky's landmark 1979 film *Stalker* and anticipated the aesthetics of Jeff VanderMeer's *Southern Reach* series of sci-fi novels (2014–24), challenged art's conventional representation of nature and pushed viewers into a zone of uncertainty and the unknown.

In the impossible task of establishing a boundary between the intentional and the unintentional, the artistic and the natural, the synthetic and the organic, the residual and the exhibitionary, Huyghe's *Untilled* stayed with the strangeness of the current anthropogenic times, making them tangible while dispensing with mediation. Our presence, as humans and visitors, was both redundant and crucial, as it turned us into witnesses of a phenomenon of terraforming that currently dominates most processes on Earth, from the most remote areas to those within the landscapes we inhabit. As such, this experiment also challenged art's relationship to its places and logics of exhibition. While it did not create a crisis for Documenta – on the contrary, it strongly contributed to that edition's narrative and imaginary – it updated it in relation to previous artworks that engaged with ecology, such as Beuys's *7000 Oaks*, whose existence, still visible today across the streets and parks of Kassel, is associated with a single, individual artistic creator. It also paved the way for a sense of collective, chaotic and blurred creation and authorship, both artistic and curatorial, that came to dominate so much of the subsequent decade's artistic experiments.

This reflection on the threads that traverse the book's five chapters could be written and rewritten again; the book makes sense in multiple variations, for the particularities that connect these artists are not a coincidence or a fortuitous resemblance. They are just a selection of artists that have aligned their work with their concerns for a planet in change. Their work is less engaged with representing and illustrating the state of the world – with conveying information that is widely available in other forms (press, literature, cinema) – than with proposing practices and methodologies that have the potential to transform. Unquestionably, they benefit the spaces and landscapes that host them. But they also propose a transformation of art viewership and its institutional setting, inviting viewers to continue contributing to experiments and experiences that, while being rewarding, may propose new ways of collectively thinking, feeling, mourning and desiring. These are fundamental pathways to understanding ourselves differently, as individuals and as species, to make us ready for a different epoch while celebrating the artistic legacy that contributed to affirming humanity's participation in the world: a mode of practising ecology with care, responsibility, joy and invention.

Notes

FOREWORD

1   Chris Jordan, 'This Is Our Culture Turned Inside Out', Feral Atlas, n.d., https://feralatlas.supdigital.org/poster/this-is-our-culture -turned-inside-out.

INTRODUCTION

1   Lucy R. Lippard, *Overlay*, The New Press, New York, 1983, p.3.
2   Ernst Haeckel, *Generelle Morphologie der Organismen* [The General Morphology of Organisms], vol.2, Georg Reimer, Berlin, 1866, p.286.
3   During the last decade, certain concepts and definitions, which for long were widely accepted, have been questioned. Feminist and ecofeminist scholars and writers have questioned the supposed universality of the notions of 'Man' and 'Mankind', revealing how they fail to represent humankind as a whole, and exclude women and non-binary people. A noteworthy example of this pioneering awareness is Ursula K. Le Guin's article 'Introducing Myself' (1992). In parallel, there have been important moves to challenge the human within the humanities and to shift them towards less anthropocentric perspectives. These proposals often focus on life beyond the human realm, comprising animals, plants, fungi and even forests, seas or geological entities. Within the humanities and social sciences, terms such as posthuman, non-human, more-than-human or other-than-human have been widely adopted by cultural thinkers, artists, theorists and others. When referring to living beings, I tend to favour the neologism *nonhuman* (single word, not hyphenated), which becomes a concept in itself and in which the comparative, negative conceptualisation of life beyond the human (non-, more-than-, other-than-) is more nuanced. Instead, when writing about what exceeds and exists beyond the human sphere, I tend to opt for the more-than-human definition, as it assumes a surplus and excess rather than a deficiency.
4   Joseph Beuys, *Eine Partei für Tiere*, 1969. Offset print stamped with handwritten text by the artist. Edition of 20.
5   Ana Mendieta, 'Personal Writings', in Gloria Moure (ed.), *Ana Mendieta*, La Polígrafa, Barcelona, 1996, p.182.
6   Vanessa Machado de Oliveira, *Hospicing Modernity: Facing Humanity's Wrongs and the Implications for Social Activism*, North Atlantic Books, Berkeley, CA, 2021.

CHAPTER 1

1   On the subject, see Øystein Dalland, 'The Alta Case: Learning from the Errors Made in a Human Ecological Conflict in Norway', *Geoforum*, vol.14, no.2, 1983, pp 193–203.
2   On the subject, see Elizabeth A. Povinelli, 'The Normativity of Creeks', *Geontologies, A Requiem to Late Liberalism*, Duke University Press, Durham, NC, and London, 2016, pp 92–117, and Maggie Wander, '"It's Ok, We're Safe Here": The Karrabing Film Collective and Colonial Histories in Australia', *Commonwealth Essays and Studies*, 2018, http://journals .openedition.org/ces/389.
3   Tess Lea and Elizabeth A. Povinelli, 'Karrabing: An Essay in Keywords', *Visual Anthropology Review*, vol.34, issue 1, Spring 2018, pp 36–46.
4   Karrabing's exhibition history is vast. Its films and installations have been presented at the survey exhibition *Night Fishing with Ancestors* at CCA Goldsmiths in London (Winter 2023–4); *Saltwater Dreams*, a film retrospective, was held at Tate Modern, London (Autumn 2017); there was an important US museum exhibition of its work at MoMA PS1 in New York (Spring 2019); and its work was included in Documenta 14 in Kassel (2022), the Jakarta Biennale (2017) and the Sydney Biennale (2016), amongst others.
5   Elizabeth A. Povinelli in conversation with Kathryn Yusoff during the opening of the exhibition *Night Fishing with Ancestors*, CCA Goldsmiths, London, 6 October 2023.
6   ibid.
7   Elizabeth A. Povinelli during the Tenth Adriaan Gerbrands Lecture, Research Center for Material Culture, Leiden, 4 March 2021.
8   ibid.
9   *Cousins and Kin*, SFCinematheque, San Francisco, 2021, https://www .sfcinematheque.org/screening/cousins-and-kin-what-was-always -yours-and-never-lost/.
10 'Conversations Between: Sky Hopinka and Theo Anthony Discuss *małni – towards the ocean, towards the shore*', *Filmmaker*, Spring 2021, https://filmmakermagazine.com/111514-conversations-between-sky -hopinka-and-theo-anthony-in-conversation-about-malni-towards -the-ocean-towards-the-shore/.
11 Machado de Oliveira, *Hospicing Modernity*, op.cit., p.xxi.
12 Sápmi is the name for the region traditionally inhabited by the Indigenous Sámi people in the north of Europe. Coinciding with other national and cultural demarcations, Sápmi comprises northern areas of Norway, Sweden, Finland and of the Kola Peninsula in Russia.
13 See Jennifer Rankin, 'Why a Swedish Town Is on the Move – One Building at a Time', *The Guardian*, 5 February 2023, https://www.theguardian.com /world/2023/feb/05/why-a-swedish-town-is-on-the-move-one-building -at-a-time-kirkuna-arctic-circle.
14 'Britta Marakatt-Labba Shares more Detail on the Replica of *Garjját / The Crows*', video made to accompany the exhibition *Under the Vast Sky*, IKON Gallery, Birmingham, 2022, https://www.facebook.com/watch /?v=3115071302087267.

15 Anders Kreuger, 'Britta Marakatt-Labba: Images Are Always Stories', *Afterall*, vol.45, Spring / Summer 2018, p.10.

16 'The Norwegian Art Scene Must Be Decolonised – Katya García-Antón interviewed by Susan Falkenås', *Kunstkritikk*, 13 November 2017.

CHAPTER 2

1 For an anthology of Earth and Land Art, see Jeffrey Kastner and Brian Wallis (eds), *Land and Environmental Art*, Phaidon, London and New York, 1998.

2 Lucy R. Lippard, *Overlay – Contemporary Art and the History of Prehistory*, Pantheon Books, New York, 1983, p.5.

3 Literally meaning 'the way of the peasant', La Via Campesina is an international network of peasants, landless workers, Indigenous people, pastoralists, fishers, migrant farmworkers, small and medium-size farmers, rural women and peasant youth founded in 1993. It defends peasant agriculture and the concept of Food Sovereignty, which champions the right to healthy and sustainable food and the right for people to define their own food and agriculture systems.

4 Fernando García-Dory, 'A Shepherds' School as a Micro Kingdom of Utopia', *Common*, Collection of Minds Issue #2, 2010.

5 Both quotes from Fernando García-Dory, 'Practice 06', in Fumihiko Sumitomo (ed.), *Foodscape: We Are What We Eat*, Anonima-Studio, Tokyo, 2016, p.64.

6 Amayuelas de Abajo has provided, since the 1990s, an example of ecological and sustainable requalification, being considered an Ecological Municipality. It progressed from its desertification and loss of juridical personhood (with the closure of the municipality in 1971) to regain civic and productive life thanks to regional social and productive activities that reutilised idle local resources while remaining respectful of the natural environment.

7 https://documenta-fifteen.de/en/lumbung-members-artists/inland/.

8 See the analysis of Norwegian sociologist and Heritage Studies research professor at the Norwegian Institute for Cultural Heritage Research, Joar Skrede, 'The Issue of Sustainable Urban Development in a Neoliberal Age – Discursive Entanglements and Disputes', *Form Academisk*, vol.6, no.1, 2013, pp 1–15.

9 Bjørvika Utvikling's interest in supporting long-lasting initiatives is likewise evident in the commission of Katie Paterson's *Future Library*. The Scottish artist created a 100-year public artwork that, from 2014 to 2114, will commission a popular author to write an original work for the project. In parallel, 1000 trees have been planted and will generate the paper upon which, in 2114, the original, unpublished manuscripts will be printed.

10 https://flatbreadsociety.net/about.

11 Emerging from the experience of *Flatbread Society*, between 2016 and 2017, Futurefarmers embarked on a *Seed Journey*, in which they travelled by boat from Oslo to Istanbul carrying the old cereal grains found in Oslo all the way to the Middle East, from where they originated. The journey was partially made on board the RS-10 *Christiania*, an 1895 wooden rescue sailboat designed by Colin Archer.

12 Amy Franceschini in conversation with Claire Doherty, in Claire Doherty (ed.), *Out of Time, Out of Place: Public Art (Now)*, Art / Books, London, 2015, p.159.

13 cf., for instance, Sam Thorne's curated exhibition *As Above, So Below: Portals, Visions, Spirits & Mystics* at the Irish Museum of Modern Art (2017); Mariana Sanchez Salvador and Rain Wu's video *As Above, So Below* (2020); Jenna Sutela's edited section 'As Above, So Below' of the book *Vita Nova* (Bom Dia Boa Tarde Boa Noite, Porto, 2021); Ignota's event *As Above, So Below* at Kings College London (2023), just to name a few.

14 Tabita Rezaire, 'Decolonial Healing: In Defense of Spiritual Technologies', *Conscience u.terre.ine*, Les Presses du réel, Paris, 2022, p.155.

15 Tabita Rezaire interviewed by Theresa Sigmund, *Contemporary And*, 13 May 2022, https://contemporaryand.com/magazines/tabita-rezaire -i-prefer-to-stand-for-things-i-believe-in/.

16 ibid.

CHAPTER 3

1 Mårten Spångberg (ed.), *The Swedish Dance History*, Inpex, Stockholm, 2011, p.9.

2 Mårten Spångberg, *The Climate The Worry The Dance*, Galeria Municipal do Porto, Porto, 2022, p.89.

3 Ann Halprin, 'Lecture on Dance Deck', Summer Workshop, 18 June 1960, Series XII, Box 5, Folder 42, AH Papers. Published in Ninotchka Bennahum, 'Anna Halprin's Radical Body in Motion', in Ninotchka Bennahum, Wendy Perron and Bruce Robertson (eds), *Radical Bodies – Anna Halprin, Simone Forti, and Yvonne Rainer in California and New York, 1955–1972*, University of California Press, Santa Barbara, CA, 2017, p.75.

4 For a detailed analysis of the environmental sensibility and concerns in the Bauhaus movement, and its connection to ecology and science, see Peder Anker, 'The Bauhaus of Nature', *Modernism / modernity*, vol.12, no.2, April 2005, pp 229–51.

5 Simone Forti (signed as Morris), *5 Pieces: Dance Report, Dance Report, Dance Construction, Dance Construction, Instructions for a Dance*, 1961, in La Monte Young and Jackson Mac Low (eds), *An Anthology of chance operations, concept art, anti art, indeterminacy, plans of action, diagrams, music, dance constructions, improvization, meaningless work, natural disasters, compositions, mathematics, essays, poetry*, Jackson Mac Low, New York, 1963.

6 *Kochi Ocean – sketches and notes* was first presented on 13 December 2016 during the Kochi-Muziris Biennale and held in the open air, at Vasco da Gama Square by the waterside in the historical centre of Kochi. *Ocean – sketches and notes* was subsequently presented at the Augarten, the former exhibition space of the TBA21 Foundation in Vienna on 23 June 2017, and at the Sequences Art Festival in Reykjavík on 8 October 2017. Jonas then presented the performance under its current title, *Moving Off the Land II*, at Tate Modern, London, on 31 May 2018; at the Ocean Space, Venice, on 7 March 2019, to coincide with the opening of the 58th Venice Biennale; and at the Prado Museum in Madrid on 27 February 2020.

7   Exhibitionary is a term coined by cultural theorist Tony Bennett in his essay 'The Exhibitionary Complex', *new formations*, no.4, Spring 1988, pp 73–102. This essay, and the definition it proposed, associated the growth and consolidation of public and private museums throughout the 19th century with the regulation (and self-regulation) of Western society. According to Bennett, museums were vital for the manufacturing and diffusion of ideals of civilisation, order and instruction, associating them with civic and political values concerned with colonialism, imperialism and nation-building. As such, they were fundamental tools of consent and uniformisation. In this book, the use of the term exhibitionary acknowledges Bennett's legacy and the ways it came to define generic practices and modalities of exhibiting.

8   Quoted from http://www.artnet.com/artists/joan-jonas/.

9   Joan Jonas, 'The Process Behind Joan Jonas' New Oceanic Work', *Flash Art*, no.326, June–August 2019.

10 Stefanie Hessler, 'Joan Jonas: Moving Off the Land II', in *Joan Jonas: Moving Off the Land II*, Museo Nacional Thyssen-Bornemisza, Madrid, 2020, p.5.

11 In 2013 *Have a Good Day!* was awarded the Globe Teana-Theatre Observation prize. In 2014 it received the Golden Stage Cross prize for the best Lithuanian Authors' Performance and the Main Prize of the Far Forward festival in Braunschweig.

12 Haley Weiss, 'Eduardo Navarro in Orbit', *Interview Magazine*, 18 July 2016, https://www.interviewmagazine.com/art/eduardo-navarro.

13 All quotes from the artist are from Justo Barranco, 'Eduardo Navarro, el artista que quiso ser foca', *La Vanguardia*, 7 April 2024 (author's translation), https://www.lavanguardia.com/cultura/20240407/9589483/artista-quiso-foca.html.

CHAPTER 4

1   The term 'attunement' follows anthropologist Tim Ingold's classification of two complementary modalities of attention that reconnect perception and imagination: attunement and exposure. By attunement, a term Ingold uses copiously, he means to be connected to the conditions of the present, to meet the world: 'not of coming up with some exact match or simulacrum for what we find in the things and happenings going on around us, but of answering to them with interventions, questions and responses of our own'. Tim Ingold, *Correspondences*, Polity, London, 2020, p.80.

2   Karen Barad, *Meeting the Universe Halfway. Quantum Physics and the Entanglement of Matter and Meaning*, Duke University Press, Durham, NC, 2007, p.ix.

3   In their paper 'Extended Spider Cognition', biologists Hilton F. Japyassú and Kevin N. Laland argue that 'web threads and configurations are integral parts of the [spiders'] cognitive systems'. In *Animal Cognition*, vol.20, 2017, pp 375–95.

4   On the topic, see Filipa Ramos, 'Uprooted: The Dramatic Performance of Plants in Museums', in *Végétal*, Chaumet, Paris, 2022, pp 165–73.

5   Evan Ziporyn, 'The Spider's Canvas', in *Arachnophilia with Evan Ziporyn*, https://arachnophilia.net/on-air-with-concerts/.

6   For more information and figures, see the British Association of Leading Visitor Attractions, https://www.alva.org.uk/details.cfm?p=423.

7   Data available at https://www.thames21.org.uk/.

8   The Maunsell Forts are a set of very imposing defensive towers that were built in the Thames and Mersey estuaries during the Second World War.

9   In 2023, the Institut Ramon Llull – a consortium made up of the Generalitat de Catalunya, the Government of the Balearic Islands, the City Council of Barcelona and the City Council of Palma – launched an open call for the artistic and curatorial proposal to represent Catalonia at the 60th Venice Biennale. *Bestiari*, the project that was selected, was a joint proposal made by artist Carlos Casas and myself, as curator of the project. Pol Capdevila was appointed curator of public programmes.

10 Barad, *Meeting the Universe Halfway*, op.cit., p.xx.

CHAPTER 5

1   Carolyn Christov-Bakargiev, in Documenta 13 press release, 2012.

2   Anselm Franke, 'Introduction', *Animism*, Haus der Kulturen der Welt, Berlin, 2012, p.10.

3   Christov-Bakargiev, Documenta 13 press release, 2012, p.5.

4   ibid., p.15.

5   Animacy begins in language. In order to challenge its naturalised hierarchies, I am extending human pronouns to this dog, who has a name and is crucial for this artwork, not so much as an attempt to attribute to them a gender but to acknowledge, and call for the recognition of, her personhood.

6   See Maria Chehonadskhih, 'dOCUMENTA (13) and the Blind Horror of the Meteorite's Point of View', *Moscow Art Magazine*, no.3, 2014, https://moscowartmagazine.com/issue/44/article/892.

7   Filipa Ramos, *Animals*, Whitechapel Gallery, London, and MIT Press, New York, 2017, p.12.

8   Marie France Rafael, *Pierre Huyghe: On Site*, Buchhandlung Walther König, Cologne, 2013, p.19.

9   Michel Foucault, 'Preface', *The Order of Things* (1966), Routledge, London, 2005, p.xix.

10 Michel Foucault, 'Of Other Spaces: Utopias and Heterotopias', (1967), *Architecture / Mouvement / Continuité*, October 1984, translated by Jay Miskowiec, pp 2–3, https://web.mit.edu/allanmc/www/foucault1.pdf.

11 ibid., p.6.

12 ibid.

13 Entomophobia, from the Greek *entomon*, insect, and *phobos*, fear, also known as insectophobia, describes the excessive and unrealistic fear and disgust experienced in relation to insects.

14 On the topic, see Meghan Bartels, 'Surprising Creatures Lurk in the Great Pacific Garbage Patch', *Scientific American*, 17 April 2023, https://www.scientificamerican.com/article/surprising-creatures-lurk -in-the-great-pacific-garbage-patch/.

15 Anna Lowenhaupt Tsing, Jennifer Deger, Alder Keleman Saxena and Feifei Zhou, *Field Guide to the Patchy Anthropocene: The New Nature*, Stanford University Press, Stanford, CA, 2024, p.48.

16 *Hyundai Commission: Anicka Yi at Tate Modern*, https://www.youtube.com /watch?v=6wyRHfImk3s.

17 See Michelle Bastian and Thom van Dooren, 'The New Immortals: Immortality and Infinitude in the Anthropocene', *Environmental Philosophy*, vol.14, no.1, January 2017, pp 1–9.

18 Hito Steyerl, 'Is a Museum a Factory?', *e-flux journal*, no.7, June–August 2009, https://www.e-flux.com/journal/07/61390/is-a-museum-a-factory/#.

19 The phrase 'every machine was once an animal' is a reference to Ben Marcus's 'Every word was once an animal', which he uses as epigraph to his book *The Age of Wire and String*, Flamingo, London, 1995.

CONCLUSION

1 Christov-Bakargiev, Documenta 13 press release, 2012.

2 See Lowenhaupt Tsing et al., *Field Guide to the Patchy Anthropocene*, op.cit.

3 Adam Tooze, 'Welcome to the World of the Polycrisis', *Financial Times*, 28 October 2022, https://www.ft.com/content/498398e7-11b1-494b-9cd3 -6d669dc3de33.

4 Machado de Oliveira, *Hospicing Modernity*, op.cit.

5 ibid., p.xxii.

6 Robert Delany, 'Sky Hopinka: The Split Tooth Interview', *Split Tooth*, 1 March 2022, https://www.splittoothmedia.com/sky-hopinka/.

7 Conversation with the author, 13 July 2024.

Further Reading

Bridle, James, *Ways of Being: Animals, Plants, Machines: The Search for a Planetary Intelligence*, London: Penguin, 2022.

Brown, Andrew, *Art & Ecology Now*, London: Thames and Hudson, 2014.

Coccia, Emanuele, *Metamorphoses*, Cambridge: Polity, 2021.

Cull Ó Maoilearca, Laura and Florence Fitzgerald-Allsopp, *Interspecies Performance*, Ceredigion, Wales: Performance Research Books, 2024.

Davis, Heather and Etienne Turpin, *Art in the Anthropocene: Encounters Among Aesthetics, Politics, Environments and Epistemologies*, London: Open Humanities Press, 2015.

Demos, T.J., *Decolonizing Nature – Contemporary Art and the Politics of Ecology*, Berlin: Sternberg Press, 2016.

Dietachmair, Philipp, Pascal Gielen and Georgia Nicola, *Sensing Earth: Cultural Quests Across a Heated Globe*, Amsterdam: Valiz, 2023.

Fowkes, Maja and Reuben Fowkes, *Art and Climate Change*, London: Thames & Hudson, 2022.

Howe, Cymene and Anand Pandian (eds), *Anthropocene Unseen, A Lexicon*, Punctum Books, 2020.

Ingold, Tim, *Imagining for Real: Essays on Creation, Attention and Correspondence*, Abingdon: Routledge, 2022.

Latour, Bruno, *Where to Land*, Cambridge: Polity, 2018.

Lavery, Carl (ed.), *Performance and Ecology: What Can Theatre Do?*, Abingdon: Routledge, 2018.

Lekkerkerk, Niekolaas Johannes and Eva Burgering, *Worlding Ecologies: Art, Science and Activism Towards Climate Justice*, Amsterdam: Valiz, 2024.

Myvillages (Kathrin Böhm, Wapke Feenstra and Antje Schiffers) (eds), *The Rural*, London: MIT Press and Whitechapel Gallery, 2020.

Tsing, Anna Lowenhaupt, Heather Swanson, Elaine Gan and Nils Bubandt (eds), *Arts of Living on a Damaged Planet*, Minneapolis, MN: University of Minnesota Press, 2017.

Weintraub, Linda, *To Life! Eco Art in Pursuit of a Sustainable Planet*, Berkeley, CA: University of California Press, 2012.

Index

*Note: italic page numbers indicate figures;
page numbers followed by n refer
to notes.*

Aboriginal people 15–16, 25–6
  see also Karrabing Film Collective
Alta River protests (Norway) 20, *21*, 36
Amakaba 17, *17*, 57, 58–60, *58*, 61, 128
Amayuelas de Abajo (Spain) 48,
  134 n.6
Ambisonics 95, 99, 130
animal rights 45, 46, 97
Animism (Franke, 2010–12) 104
Anthropocene 9, 114–15, 124
Anthropocene Curriculum, The
  (HKW, 2013–22) 83–4, 116
anthropocentrism 48, 65, 77, 93, 97, 98
anthropology 29, 30, 116
Arachnophilia community 18, 83, 88–90
assemblages 51–2, 66, 103, 108, 114, 129
astronomy 14, 82
Australia *see* Aboriginal people
Barad, Karen 85, 101
Barzdžiukaitė, Rugilė 17–18, 63, 71–4,
  71, 79
beluga whale 69–70
Bestiari (Casas, 2024) 18, 96–9, *97*
Beuys, Joseph 14, 108, 131
Biennale Gherdëina 59
biodiversity 7, 46
Bohr, Niels 85
Bourriaud, Nicolas 114, 115
Carson, Rachel 65, 68
Casas, Carlos 18, 81–2, 96–101, *97*
CAST (Center for Art, Science
  and Technology, Massachusetts
  Institute of Technology) 83
Chacon, Raven 33
Chernobyl disaster (1986) 15
Christov-Bakargiev, Carolyn 102, 104,
  105, 110, 123, 124, 130

climate change 7, 13, 18, 71, 73, 114
coexistence 22, 45, 58, 73, 85
Colectivo Los Ingrávidos 33
colonialism 22, 23, 26, 29, 30, 31, 35,
  39, 57
COUSIN collective 16, 22–3, 24, 31–5,
  38, 127–8, 129
  and audience 32–3
  and decolonisation 39, 40
  and indigeneity 31
  as Indigenous cinema
  movement 32
COVID-19 pandemic 74, 76, 128
dance 62, 63, 64–5, 79, 105
decolonisation 39–40, 104, 128
Disputa de l'ase (Turmeda) 96, 98
Documenta 14, 38, 50, 133 n.4
Documenta 13 102–12, 124
  and *Animism* 104
  and dance 105–6
  and Huyghe 18, 106–12, *107*,
  130, 131
  sites of 103–4, 106, 111
ecology 10–13
  and contemporary art 12–14
  Haeckel's definition of 10–12
  as movement of resistance 12
embroidery 16, 23, 24, 36, 37–8,
  37, 40
entanglements 26, 48, 84–5
environmental justice 13, 16, 22, 83
exhibitions 18–19, 31, 40, 62, 101,
  102, 112–14
  and industrial spaces 120–21
  see also specific exhibitions / museums
extinctions 13, 98
extraction / extractivism 10, 13, 25–6,
  31, 35, 66, 98, 100
farming / pastoralism 7, 16–17, *17*, 41,
  44–7, 60–61
  and animal rights 45, 46

and co-evolution 46
industrial 42, 58
see also Amakaba; Futurefarmers;
    INLAND
feminism 14, 57, 58, 59, 70, 85,
    132 n.3
Feral Atlas 7, 19, 115–18, *116–17*,
    122–3, 124
film 7, 14–16, 23, 24, 96
see also COUSIN collective;
    Karrabing Film Collective
Flatbread Society (Futurefarmers)
    53–6, *53*, 61, 92, 134 n.11
F.O.C.A. project (Navarro) 18, 76–8,
    77, 79
Folkeaksjonen (protest movement) 20
Forti, Simone 64, *64*, 65
Foucault, Michel 110–11
Franceschini, Amy 51, 54
Franke, Anselm 104, 109–10
French Guiana 17, *17*, 57, 58–60, 128
Futurefarmers 16–17, 51–6, *53*, 60
Flatbread Society 53–6, *53*, 61, 92,
    134 n.11
García-Dory, Fernando 16, 44–5,
    46–7, 49, 50, 60, 106
Grainytė, Vaiva 17–18, 63, 71–4,
    71, 79
Grandin, Temple 129
Great Pacific Garbage Patch 114
grief 125–6
Group 'I' 15
Gwangju Biennale 28
Haeckel, Ernst 10–12, *11*
Halprin, Anna 64–5, *64*, 79
heterotopias 110–11
HKW (Haus der Kulturen der Welt,
    Berlin) 83–4, *84*, 116
Ho-Chunk Nation 32, 33
Holt, Nancy 14
Hopinka, Sky 22, 32, 33–4, *34*,
    127–8
Huyghe, Pierre 18, 88, 106–14,
    107, 122–3, 130–131
identity 10, 15, 51
and Indigenous people 16, 22, 23,
    24, 31, 39, 40
Indigenous justice 16
Indigenous knowledge 7–8, 22, 59–60

Indigenous peoples 15–16, 20–40,
    42, 86
and colonialism 22, 23, 26, 29,
    30, 31, 35
and identity *see under* identity
and land rights 21–2, 23, 25
and language 15, 23, 25, 33
see also Aboriginal people;
    Sámi people
INLAND (farmers' community) 16,
    47–51, *49*, 61
installation 17, 19, 26, 31, 75
sonic 18, 88–9, 92, 93–6, 129
interconnection 15, 56, 66, 124–5, 135
    n.13
interspecies relations 18, 36, 82, 91–2,
    96, 99
Istanbul Biennial 19, 114–18, *116–17*
Jonas, Joan 17, 63, 65–70, *68*, 79,
    106, 129
Jordan, Chris 7
Karlsaue Park (Kassel, Germany) 104,
    106, 111
Karrabing Film Collective 15–16, 22,
    23–4, 25–31, *27*, 37
and colonialism 22, 26, 29, 30, 31
and decolonisation 39
and distortions / deconstructions
    29–31
and exhibitions 29, 31, 133 n.4
formation of 25–6
and improvisational realism 28–9
output / subject matter of 26–8
and videoclips 27–8
Kassel (Germany) 14, 18, 50, 103–4,
    131
see also Documenta
Kawaguchi, Tatsuo 15
Khalil, Adam 22, 32, 34–5, 40
Kitakyushu Project Gallery (Japan) 66
Kochi-Muziris Biennale (Kerala,
    India) 66
Kreuger, Anders 36
La Via Campesina 44, 134 n.3
landscapes 21, 23, 24, 30, 37, 38, 42
language 15, 19, 23, 25, 33, 42
Lapelytė, Lina 17–18, 63, 71–4, *71*, 79
Lazarowich, Alexandra 23, 32
Leath, A.A. 64, *64*

Leeum Museum (Seoul) 119, *119*
Lippard, Lucy 9, 43, 56
local contexts / practices 40, 44, 45,
    46, 47, 53, 59, 83
Lucier, Alvin 89–90
Machado de Oliveira, Vanessa 19, 35,
    125, 126
Madrid (Spain) 44, 48, 49
Marakatt-Labba, Britta 16, 20–21, 23,
    24, 35–9, *37*, 40, *126–7*
    and Alta River protest 36
    and spirituality 36–7
Martínez, Chus 102
Mázejoavku (Máze Group) 20–1, 24, 36
Mendieta, Ana 14–15
modernity 12, 19, 26, 35, 98, 104,
    114, 125
more-than-human 44, 74, 81, 82, 93
music 18, 24, 33, 39, 68, 71–3, 80, 81,
    83, 89–92
National Gallery of Art (Vilnius) 72
Natural History Museum (London)
    18, 92, 93, 95–6, 122, 129
nature
    and agency 65, 69–70
    dominance / exploitation of 9–10
    separated from humans 12, 14, 19
    shared rights with people 15, 23
Navarro, Eduardo 18, 63, 74–8, *77*,
    79, 128–9
New Museum Triennale 129
nonhuman 12, 18, 23, 27, 45, 46, 48,
    65, 129, 132 n.3
Norway 20–21, *21*, 24, 37, 39, 53–4,
    53, 92
    see also Oslo
oceans 17, 66–70, 72
O'Doherty, Brian 88, 106
On Air exhibition (Saraceno, 2018–19)
    84–8
Oslo (Norway) 53–4, *53*, 55, 134 n.11
Painlevé, Jean 66
Palais de Tokyo (Paris) 84–8, 113
Pechanga Band of Luiseño people
    32, 33
performance 14–15, 17–18, 62–3, 65,
    66–74, 76–8, 105
    opera- 71–4
Phan, Thao Nguyen 66

Pietroiusti, Lucia 71
Piron, Adam 23, 32
plastic 7, 94, 98, 114
pollution 7, 13, 94, 114
polycrisis 124–5
Pompidou Centre (Paris) 88, 109
Povinelli, Elizabeth A. 28, 30, 31
prehistoric art 9, 43
Radigue, Élaine 90
Ramos, Filipa 7, 8
Rezaire, Tabita *17*, 56–60, 61, 128
rituals 9, 24, 35, 37, 52, 56, 57
River, The (Winderen) 18, 93–6, *94*,
    99–101, 129
Rural Art, Commission for 44, 47
rural context / practices 40, 41–2, 43
    see also farming / pastoralism
Rural Platform 44, 46, 47
Sámi Dáiddajoavku (Sámi Artists'
    Group) 36
Sámi people 16, 20–21, 24, 35, 38–9
    and Sápmi region 23, 35, 36, 38,
    133 n.12
    and shamanism 36–7, 38
    storytelling tradition of 38
    see also Marakatt-Labba, Britta;
    Máze Group
Saraceno, Tomás 18, 81–92, *84*,
    99–101, 113
    On Air exhibition (2018–19) 84–8
science 10–12, 26, 58, 69, 82, 83, 85,
    91, 103, 123
sculpture 14, 65, 75
seal rescue 7, 18, 76–8, *77*, 128–9
Sehgal, Tino 105–6
shamanism 36–7, 38
Sharjah Biennial 19
Shepherds' School (Spain) 44–6, 49
Sherk, Bonnie Ora 14
Smithsonian Institution
    (Washington DC) 122
social justice 13, 23, 83
song 28, 71–4
SOS Rescate Fauna Marina
    (Uruguay) 76
sound 18, 28, 30, 50, 68, 75, 80,
    81–101, 129–130
    and spiders' webs 82–4, 88–92
Spain 16, 44–5, 46, 47, 48, 49, 96–7

Spångberg, Mårten 62, 63
Spider/Web Research Group 82–3
spiders' webs 7, 18, 82–92
    and *On Air* exhibition (2018–19)
    84–8
    and sound / music 82–4, 88–92
    and structure of the cosmos 82, 91
spirituality 15, 36–7, 56–7, 58, 59,
    60, 86, 128
Stalker (Tarkovsky, 979) 107–8, 130
Steyerl, Hito 120–121
storytelling 24, 27–8, 31, 38, 40,
    98, 117
Sun & Sea (Marina) (Barzdžiukaitė /
    Grainytė / Lapelytė, 2019) 17–18,
    71–4, *71*, 79
Sweden 16, 24
Sweitzer, Bayley 34–5, 40
Tarkovsky, Andrei 107–8, 130
Tate Modern (London) 19, 67, 96,
    118–20, 121, 123
TBA21–Academy 66, 67
Thames, River 93–6, *94*, 129
theatre 62, 70, 71, 72, 73, 74
Tooze, Adam 124–5

tree-planting 14, 108, 134 n.9
Tsing, Anna Lowenhaupt 19, 116,
    117, 124
Turmeda, Anselm 96, 98
United States (US) 16–17, 64
    see also COUSIN collective
Untilled (Huyghe, 2011–12) 18, 106–8,
    107, 110, 111, 114, 130–131
    see also Way in Untilled, A
Uruguay 18, 76, 128, 129
Van Dessel, Marthe 51, 54
Venice Biennale 17–18, 71, 72, 73, 74,
    96, 119
video installations 23, 28, 57, 59–60, 65
videoclips 27–8
Visions of Nature (Natural History
    Museum, 2024–ongoing) 122
Vranken, Lode 51, 54
weaving *see* embroidery
Winderen, Jana 18, 81–2, 92–6, *94*,
    99–101, 129
wolves 46
Yi, Anicka 19, 118–23, *119*
Zhou, Feifei *116–17*, 117–18, 123
Ziporyn, Evan 90

Image Credits

Acknowledgements

This book would not exist were it not for the invitation of the series editor, Marcus Verhagen. I am grateful for his support and encouragement, and for trusting that a book highlighting the brighter sides of environmental artivism was necessary and urgent. I am likewise grateful to editor Lucy Myers, whose keen eye, curious mind and patience accompanied me throughout the writing and editing process, and to copy editor Michela Parkin, who mended my English with the precision and care of a Kintsugi Master.

Haus der Kunst's Director, Andrea Lissoni, was the original manuscript's first (and sole) reader. His feedback on both major questions and minor details was invaluable. Chus Martínez, Director of the Art Institute at the FHNW Academy of Art and Design, Basel, where I teach, created the best writing conditions possible, offering me trust, professional exchange and research time.

I would likewise thank Alejandro Cesarco at the Malmö Art Academy; Milena Høgsberg at Wanås Konst; Andrés Jaque at Columbia University Graduate School of Architecture, Planning and Preservation; Alex Jordan and Anja Wegner at the Max Plank Institute of Animal Behaviour; Steven Madoff at the New York School of Visual Arts; Godofredo Pereira at Environmental Architecture at the Royal College of Art; and the team of the Institute for Postnatural Studies for inviting me to present the research associated with this book during talks, lectures and academic seminars.

I thank all the incredible artists and curators whose work is featured here and am grateful for the time, trust and opportunities many of them gave me. They continue to provide outstanding examples of how art can and should participate in and contribute to the betterment of the more-than-human world.

While writing this book, Meo, my beloved friend, writing companion and birdwatching buddy, passed away. This book is dedicated to him.